fishamble
THE NEW PLAY COMPANY

PRESENTS

RANK

ROBERT MASSEY

T0347683

Fishamble Theatre Company is funded by the Arts Council / An Chomhairle Ealaíon and Dublin City Council.

THEATRE FORUM MEMBER
The Voice of the Performing Arts

culture **ireland**
cultúr **éireann**

promoting the arts abroad
ag cur chun cinn na n-ealaíon thar lear

Dublin City
Baile Átha Cliath

the **arts**
council
an chomhairle
ealaíon

FISHAMBLE

Staff

Artistic Director	Jim Culleton
General Manager	Orla Flanagan
Literary Manager	Gavin Kostick

Board

Eoin Kennelly (Chair)
Siobhan Maguire
Stuart McLaughlin
Jo Mangan
Vincent O'Doherty
Andrew Parkes

Fishamble wishes to thank the following Friends of Fishamble for their invaluable support:

Robert & Lillian Chambers
Helen Cunningham
Brian Friel
Marian Keyes
Jo Mangan
Vincent O'Doherty
Andrew & Delyth Parkes
Michael & Mary O'Connor
John McColgan & Moya Doherty
David and Veronica Rowe
Dearbhail Ann Shannon

Thank you also to those who do not wish to be credited.

For details on how to become a Friend of Fishamble please see www.fishamble.com **or email** orla@fishamble.com

Fishamble also wishes to thank the following for their support with *Rank*:

John O'Kane, David Parnell and all at the Arts Council, Jack Gilligan and all at Dublin City Council Arts Office, Eugene Downes, Christine Sisk and all at Culture Ireland, Loughlin Deegan, Triona Ni Dhuibhir, Stephen McManus and all at the Ulster Bank Dublin Theatre Festival, Una Carmody and all at the Helix, Brid Dukes and all at the Civic, Nicolas Kent, Mary Lauder and all at the Tricycle Theatre, The Carlton Hotel, Elaine Martin, Gerry McCann, Rory Nolan, Caroline Gray, Louise Lowe and all those who have helped Fishamble with the production since this publication went to print.

Fishamble: The New Play Company

Shamrock Chambers
1/2 Eustace Street
Dublin 2
Ireland
Tel: +353-1-670 4018
Fax: +353-1-670 4019
E-mail: info@fishamble.com
Website: www.fishamble.com

RANK

BY ROBERT MASSEY

Rank was first produced by **Fishamble: The New Play Company**.
The production opened on 2 October 2008 at the Helix,
as part of the Ulster Bank Dublin Theatre Festival.

**The performance runs for 2 hours including one interval.
The play is set in the present in Dublin.**

Cast (in order of appearance)

Jack Farrell	**Bryan Murray**
Fred Farrell	**Luke Griffin**
Carl Conway	**Alan King**
George Kelly	**Eamonn Hunt**
'Two in the Bush'	**John Lynn**

Director	**Jim Culleton**
Set & Costume Designer	**Blaithin Sheerin**
Lighting Designer	**Mark Galione**
Sound Designers	**Ivan Birthistle & Vincent Doherty**
Fight Coordinator	**Paul Burke**
Producers	**Orla Flanagan, Marketa Puzman**
Dramaturg	**Gavin Kostick**
Production Manager	**Des Kenny**
Stage Director	**Marketa Puzman**
Stage Manager	**Clive Welsh**
Marketing & Publicity	**Highlight Productions**
Graphic Design	**Gareth Jones**
Photography	**Patrick Redmond**
Assistant Director	**Louise Lowe**
Costume Assistant	**Caroline Gray**

Rank runs at the Helix (30 September–11 October), the Civic Theatre, Tallaght
(13-18 October) and the Tricycle Theatre, London (3–22 November).

ARTISTIC LICENCE

Dermot Bolger

This year marks the twentieth anniversary of the real millennium. I don't mean the minor sideshow of 2000, based on the unproven date of Christ's birth and dodgy rumours of a millennium bug that allowed computer experts to build conservatories with over-time payments. I refer to the millennium of 1988 when Dublin's City Fathers decreed that in 988 the Vikings – bored of battering lice-infected Celts in local metropolises like Finglas – had reclaimed the Liffey swamplands and started building Dublin.

Having spent a thousand years vainly trying to finish the job, the City Fathers were determined in 1988 that we celebrate Dublin's birth. A host of worthy cultural initiatives were unleashed. Some had lasting effect, though my favourite was the millennium milk bottle, resplendent with a coloured city crest and delivered to every household to be passed down to future generations as a family heirloom.

But no official initiative taken that year had a more lasting impact than the initiative shown by a handful of young people – led by Jim Culleton, Kathy Downes and Paul Hickey – who began staging drama in the tiny Players Theatre in Trinity College in 1988. Initially calling themselves Pigsback, they soon moved to the old Project Art Centre and unleashed *Don Juan* – the first of Michael West's riotous adaptations of European classics – upon the unsuspecting Irish public. Inventive, boisterous and played with an energy that made the Project no place for anyone with a pacemaker; West's adaptations for Pigsback – especially *The Tender Trap* – remain vivid today.

The old Project (with buckets suspended from the ceiling to collect rainwater – which some patrons mistook for an artistic installation) became a remarkable cradle of talent as Fishamble – as they were now called – made their core policy the instigation of original Irish drama.

I vividly recall the wondrous experience of seeing Gavin Kostick's *The Ash Fire* in 1992, which showed the European Jewish emigrant experience taking root within the new housing estates of Cabra. A period play about the future, it provided a foretaste of life for the generation of immigrants growing up here today, caught between their parents' experiences and their new lives in Ireland.

I recall the same theatre packed for *Red Roses and Petrol*, Joseph O'Connor's fine debut play which dissected the tensions and loyalties of Irish family life in a way that was lacerating, painful and richly comic. Not only were Fishamble adept at nurturing new talent, but it had an artistic director in Jim Culleton whom actors and writers would happily wade through the blood of disembowelled critics to work with.

Red Roses and Petrol gave them increased international profile, but their profile within Ireland had already been confirmed by the presence of the President, Mary Robinson, at the opening of *This Love Thing*, by the then virtually unknown Marina Carr. And Fishamble kept on unearthing new Irish talent.

Mark O'Rowe's debut, *From Both Hips,* signified the arrival of a dramatist intent on using language in a new way on the Irish stage. Underneath its humour there lurked an edge of menace poised to pounce at any moment. Pat Kinevane's *The Nun's Wood* was a stunning evocation of the cusp world of adolescence with its haunting discoveries and doubts.

Here was a company with no agenda except to be led by the imagination of its playwrights. It has continued discovering inventive voices – most recently Sean McLoughlin's superb *Noah and the Tower Flower.* But established authors love working with them too – their 2007 production of Sebastian Barry's astonishing *The Pride of Parnell Street* will not be forgotten by anyone privileged enough to see it.

For Fishamble the process starts again this autumn in the Dublin Theatre Festival, with another new play, *Rank,* a darkly comic thriller by Robert Massey. Serious theatre goers will mark it down as a must see because it is the latest in a tapestry of challenging, distinctive plays which Fishamble has given the Irish public since that summer twenty years ago when young people came together to turn a dream into reality in the tiny Players Theatre. Original art is never conjured by a committee. It comes from the creative energy of like-minded dreamers unafraid to fail as they voyage into the unknown. Good luck to Robert Massey on joining a unique crew. May *Rank* launch another twenty year voyage as exciting as the last one, as Fishamble sail on.

FISHAMBLE: THE NEW PLAY COMPANY – CELEBRATING 20 YEARS OF THEATRE!

The Company was founded in 1988 and, since 1990, has been dedicated to the discovery, development and production of new work for the Irish stage. Formerly known as Pigsback, the Company was renamed Fishamble in 1997. The name is inspired by Dublin's Fishamble Street and in particular, its playhouse which, in 1784, became the first Irish theatre to pursue a policy of producing new Irish work. Fishamble: The New Play Company has produced many plays by first-time and established playwrights in Dublin and throughout Ireland.

Fishamble's passionate commitment to new plays and new approaches to creating theatre has been demonstrated through 20 years of production and innovation. In recent years, every Fishamble project has been nominated for or received major awards and/or toured nationally and internationally.

Fishamble Firsts

The *Fishamble Firsts* scheme focuses on producing first plays by new writers. This includes recent productions such as *Noah and the Tower Flower* by Sean McLoughlin (2007) which won *The Irish Times* Best New Play Award and the Stewart Parker Trust Award, *The Gist of It* by Rodney Lee (2006) which was staged in New York by Origin/Fishamble, and *Monged* by Gary Duggan (2005) which won the Stewart Parker Trust Award, toured to Liverpool and was also staged in New York by Origin/Fishamble. Gavin Kostick, Deirdre Hines, Mark O'Rowe and Pat Kinevane also won a BBC/Stewart Parker Trust Award for their first plays, which were commissioned and produced by the Company.

International Touring

Fishamble has brought its work to the US, England, Scotland, Canada, Czech Republic, Romania, France and Germany. During 2008, Fishamble toured *The Pride of Parnell Street* by Sebastian Barry (opened at the Tricycle in London in 2007) to the Centre Culturel Irlandais (Paris), Neue Stucke Aus Europa (Wiesbaden) and Festival of Arts & Ideas (New Haven), as well as touring *Forgotten* by Pat Kinevane to the Centre Culturel Irlandais (Paris), Kostel Na Pradle (Prague), International Theatre Festival (Sibiu), Dance Base (Edinburgh) and Unity Theatre (Liverpool). *Rank* is the fifth production the Company has brought to the Tricycle.

Awards

The Company's work has won a number of awards including *The Irish Times* Theatre Awards, BBC/Stewart Parker Trust Awards, Dublin City Council Awards and *In Dublin* Theatre Awards. It has also been nominated or shortlisted for *The Irish Times* Theatre Awards, Entertainment & Media Awards, *The Irish Times* Living Dublin Awards, ZeBBie Awards and Allianz Business to Arts Awards. Recent awards include *The Irish Times* Theatre Awards for *Whereabouts* (2006 Special Judges' Award) and for *Noah and the Tower Flower* (2007 Best New Play Award), as well as nominations for *Forgotten* and *The Pride of Parnell Street.*

Publications

Fishamble frequently works with publishers, including New Island Books, Nick Hern Books, Faber & Faber and Methuen, in order to extend the life of plays beyond production. In recent years, Fishamble has published every play it premieres. In 2008, New Island Books will publish a second volume of *Fishamble Firsts* including plays by new playwrights, available in the bookshops in October.

Partnerships

Fishamble often works in partnership with arts and non-arts organisations. Recent and current partners include development agencies, venues and festivals throughout Ireland, as well as festivals, theatres and cultural centres in the UK, the US and Europe. Other partners include Amnesty International, RTÉ lyric fm, British Council Ireland, TNL Canada, Ireland Newfoundland Partnership, The Gaiety School of Acting, Business to Arts, Origin Theatre Company (New York), Allianz, National Association of Youth Drama, The Irish Council for Bioethics and Temple Bar Cultural Trust.

Training & Development

Fishamble runs many developmental initiatives and training projects, such as play development workshops, dramaturgical support, discussions, seminars, special events, and readings of commissioned and unsolicited work. The Company runs a programme of ongoing playwriting courses which are open to the public. These courses often form links with other new play companies in Ireland, the UK, Europe and the U.S.

This strand of work also includes a mentoring scheme for Youth Theatre directors run in partnership with the National Association of Youth Drama, internships run with institutions including NUI and IES, off-site playwriting courses for literary, arts and theatre festivals nationwide, corporate training initiatives delivered in partnership with Business to Arts, and the *Fishamble New Writing Award*, launched in 2007, awarded to the best new writing in the Dublin Fringe Festival.

Readings & Other Events

In tandem with its world premiere productions, Fishamble often curates and presents readings and other events that explore contemporary theatre. Recently, these events include: a reading in association with Amnesty International of *My Name is Rachel Corrie* by Rachel Corrie, Alan Rickman and Katherine Viner (2008); *55 degrees and rising* - readings of Scottish plays by Stephen Greenhorn, Zinnie Harris, David Greig and David Harrower (2005); and *Dislocated* - readings of plays by Marius Von Mayenburg, Benny McDonnell and Leo Butler (2004).

Future productions

New work currently in development includes plays by Sebastian Barry, Gary Duggan, Gavin Kostick, Sean McLoughlin and Abbie Spallen. In 2009, Fishamble will present a staged reading of Paul Meade's play, *Begotten not Made*, hosted by the BioEthics Council of Ireland, *Handel's Crossing* by Joseph O'Connor in partnership with Temple Bar Cultural Trust for the Handel 250th Anniversary, and is also developing projects with St Francis Hospice, Tinderbox and ODOS Architects.

UPCOMING PRODUCTIONS AND EVENTS

Staged Reading of New Work

As part of the Ulster Bank Dublin Theatre Festival's *In Development* series Fishamble will present a staged reading of work currently in progess, directed by Jim Culleton.

4pm, Sunday 12 October

Project Arts Centre (admission free but booking advisable, 01 677 8899)

Forgotten

Written and performed by Pat Kinevane

3 October, GAA Clubhouse, Cobh

21-22 October, Unity Theatre, Liverpool Irish Festival

5-6 November, Belltable Arts Centre, Limerick

12-13 November, Mermaid Arts Centre, Bray

> 'a consummate act of storytelling...a striking accomplishment; captivating, moving and – yes – even unforgettable.' *The Irish Times*

See www.fishamble.com for further information

PREVIOUS WORLD PREMIERES

2008
The Pride of Parnell Street by Sebastian Barry (revival)
Forgotten by Pat Kinevane (revival)

2007
The Pride of Parnell Street by Sebastian Barry
Noah and the Tower Flower by Sean McLoughlin*
Forgotten by Pat Kinevane

2006
Monged by Gary Duggan (revival)
Whereabouts by Shane Carr*, John Cronin*, John Grogan*, Louise Lowe, Belinda McKeon*, Colin Murphy*, Anna Newell*, Jack Olohan*, Jody O'Neill*, Tom Swift and Jacqueline Strawbridge* (a series of short, site-specific plays)
Forgotten by Pat Kinevane (work-in-progress)
The Gist of It by Rodney Lee*

2005
Monged by Gary Duggan*
She Was Wearing... by Sebastian Barry, Maeve Binchy, Dermot Bolger, Michael Collins, Stella Feehily, Rosalind Haslett, Roisin Ingle*, Marian Keyes* and Gavin Kostick

2004
Pilgrims in the Park by Jim O'Hanlon
Tadhg Stray Wandered In by Michael Collins

2003
Handel's Crossing by Joe O'Connor, *The Medusa* by Gavin Kostick, *Chaste Diana* by Michael West and *Sweet Bitter* by Stella Feehily (a season of radio plays)
Shorts by Dawn Bradfield*, Aino Dubrawsky*, Simon O'Gorman*, Ciara Considine*, Tina Reilly*, Mary Portser, Colm Maher*, James Heaney*, Tara Dairman*, Lorraine McArdle*, Talaya Delaney*, Ger Gleeson*, Stella Feehily* and Bryan Delaney*
The Buddhist of Castleknock by Jim O'Hanlon (revival)

2002
Contact by Jeff Pitcher and Gavin Kostick (a live, webcast, simultaneous, cross-Atlantic production)
The Buddhist of Castleknock by Jim O'Hanlon*
Still by Rosalind Haslett*

* denotes first play by a new playwright

2001
The Carnival King by Ian Kilroy*
Wired to the Moon by Maeve Binchy, adapted by Jim Culleton

2000
Y2K Festival: *Consenting Adults* by Dermot Bolger, *Dreamframe* by Deirdre Hines, *Moonlight and Music* by Jennifer Johnston, *The Great Jubilee* by Nicholas Kelly*, *Doom Raider* by Gavin Kostick, *Tea Set* by Gina Moxley

1999
The Plains of Enna by Pat Kinevane
True Believers by Joe O'Connor

1998
The Nun's Wood by Pat Kinevane*

1997
From Both Hips by Mark O'Rowe*

1996
The Flesh Addict by Gavin Kostick

1995
Sardines by Michael West
Red Roses and Petrol by Joe O'Connor*

1994
Jack Ketch's Gallows Jig by Gavin Kostick

1993
Buffalo Bill Has Gone To Alaska by Colin Teevan
The Ash Fire by Gavin Kostick (revival)

1992
The Ash Fire by Gavin Kostick*
The *Tender Trap* by Michael West

1991
Howling Moons/Silent Sons by Deirdre Hines*
This Love Thing by Marina Carr

1990
Don Juan by Michael West

CAST / PRODUCTION

Luke Griffin Fred Farrell

Theatre includes *Moving* by Hugh Leonard, *Drama At Inish* by Lennox Robinson, *On The Outside* by Tom Murphy and *Made In China* by Mark O'Rowe all at the Abbey. *Borstal Boy* by Brendan Behan, *Juno and the Paycock* by Sean O'Casey at the Gaiety. *The Lieutenant of Inishmore* by Martin McDonagh in the Garrick London. *DogShow: Shep* and *Dogshow: Fido* by Garrett Keogh and *Setanta Murphy Part One* also by Garrett Keogh. Television and films include *Pure Mule* for RTE, *Band Of Brothers* for HBO, *The Disappearance of Finbar* Samson Films, *The Nephew* for Irish Dreamtime, *Borstal Boy* for Hells Kitchen.

Eamonn Hunt George Kelly

Eamonn's most recent theatre includes Seamus Heaney's version of Sophocles' *Antigone*, *The Burial at Thebes*, Paul Mercier's *Homeland* (Abbey Theatre), *Our National Games* (axis, Ballymun), *Lizzie Lavelle* (Performance Corporation), *Stone Mad* (Everyman Palace Cork) Robert Pinget's *Night* (Kilkenny Arts Festival), Old Mahon in *The Playboy of the Western World* (Big Telly Co), *Hurl* (Barabbas), *Shorts*, *The Carnival King* and *Whereabouts* (Fishamble), *One – Healing with Theatre* (Pan Pan), *The Kings of the Kilburn High Road* (Red Kettle, Irish tour, Tricycle London and Off Broadway).

Television credits include *The Running Mate* (TG4), *Holby City* (BBC) and *The Truth About Claire*, *Glenroe*, *Fair City*, *Love is the Drug* (RTE).

Films include *Anne Devlin*, *Hard Shoulder*, *Snakes and Ladders*, *35 Aside*, *I Went Down*, *Nora*, *Saltwater*, *Agnes Browne*, *The Honeymooners*, *Inside I'm Dancing*, *Adam and Paul*, *Man About Dog*, *A Man of Few Words*, *Short Order*, *Boris*, *WC*, *Lassie*, *Studs* and *Happy Ever Afters*.

Alan King Carl Conway

Alan began his acting career with Dublin Youth Theatre and later trained at Bull Alley. He co-founded Purple Heart Theatre Company, is an associate artist of Calipo Theatre and Picture Co, a former Artistic Director of Bewley's Café Theatre and currently works for the National Association for Youth Drama as their Youth Theatre Officer. He is delighted to be working with Fishamble for the first time, on the world premiere of *Rank*.

Theatre credits include *Studs* (Tricycle, Tivoli), *Brownbread* (Olympia), *Buddleia* (Donmar Warehouse, Project) and *Diarmuid & Grainne* (Assembly Rooms, Edinburgh) all with the Passion Machine, *Brighton Beach Memoirs* and *The Stomping Ground* (Red Kettle), *Danti-Dan* (Rough Magic, Hampstead Theatre), *Mojo*, *Some Voices* (Purple Heart), *The Twits* (Civic Theatre), *Car Show 3: Generations* (Corn Exchange), *One: Healing with Theatre* (Pan Pan), *Horst Buchholz and Other Stories* (Bewley's Cafe Theatre), *From These Green Heights* (Axis Arts Centre – *The Irish Times* Awards Best Play 2004), *Green* (Vicar Street), *Wild Harvest* (Fada), *Shoot The Butterfly* (Team) and *A Few White Lies* (Andrews Lane Theatre). TV and film work includes *Inside I'm Dancing* (Working Title 2), *Salt Water* (Treasure

left to right
Luke Griffin
Eamonn Hunt
Alan King
John Lynn
Bryan Murray
Robert Massey
Jim Culleton

Films),*The Van* (Deadly Films),*The Family, Rough Diamond* and *Custers Last Stand Up* (BBC), *Before I Sleep, Studs* (Brother Films) *Love is the Drug, Fair City, Trouble in Paradise* and *An Officer from France* (RTE), *Honeymooners* (Samson Films), *Mystics* (Irish Screen), *Frankie* (Calipo Films), *Forecourt* (Parralell Films) and *Recoil* (Zanzibar Films). Radio includes: *Lennon's Guitar, The Anniversary Orchid, Metronome, Danti – Dan, Mrs. Sweeny and Close Encounters* all for RTE Radio 1.

In more recent years Alan has concentrated on directing and many highlights includes the Irish premieres of *Coyote On A Fence, Bug* and *On An Average Day (*Purple Heart Theatre Co), *The End of The Beginning, And They Used To Star in Movies*, (Bewley's Café Theatre) *Waiting for IKEA*; Nominee Fishamble New Writing Award, Nominee Bewley's Café Theatre Award at the Dublin Fringe Fest '07, and *Mind Your Fingers*, winner of Jayne Snow Award, Dublin Fringe Festival '05.

John Lynn 'Two in the Bush'

John trained for the screen with the Irish Films Actors Studio and for the stage on Dublin's gruelling profit share circuit. Film credits include Rick Larkin's feature *Satellites* and *Meteorites* for I-Wire Films due for release in 2009. Television appearances include BBC 3's *Be More Ethnic, One Night Stand* (BBC NI) as well as *The Third Policeman's Ball (*TV3) and *The Liffey Laughs* (RTE). John's last theatrical role was in Robert Massey's debut offering *Deadline*, staged by Lane Productions. Other theatre credits include *Stages*

(Civic Theatre) and *Ergophobia* (Teachers Club). John's sporadic bouts of acting unemployment are filled with performing as a stand up comedian and he has just returned from the ultra prestigious invite only Montreal Just for Laughs Comedy Festival.

Bryan Murray Jack Farrell

Bryan Murray trained at The Abbey Theatre in Dublin with the great Frank Dermody and was a member of that company for seven years. He has also been a member of The Royal Shakespeare Company and the National Theatre Company. His theatre work includes *The Plough and the Stars, Juno and the Paycock, The Shadow of a Gunman, The Silver Tassie, The Hostage, St Joan, Deathwatch, The Devils, The Glass Menagerie, Blood Wedding, Philadelphia, Here I Come!, Volunteers, The Rivals, Catchpenny Twist, Nashville New York, Miss Firecracker Contest, Blood Brothers, The Cavalcaders, Misery, Deathtrap, Boyband, An Inspector Calls, An Ideal Husband, Joe & I, Salomé, Anna Karenina, Great Expectations* and most recently *The Deep Blue Sea.*

For the past fifteen years he has worked mainly in television. He is probably best known for his roles as Fitz in *Strumpet City,* Flurry Knox in *The Irish RM*, Shifty in *Bread* (for which he won BBC TV Personality Of The Year), Harry Cassidy in *Perfect Scoundrels* and his controversial role as 'Trevor Jordache' in *Brookside* and recently 'Bob Charles' in *Fair City.* His other television appearances include *The Year of the French, I'm a Dreamer Montreal, Rifleman, Bread or Blood, Final Run, Iris in the Traffic, The Franchise*

Affair, Gates of Gold, Hard Shoulder, The Trials of Oscar Wilde, Casualty, Holby City, The Bill, Silent Witness, Proof, the ITV drama Baby War, and Golden Globe nominated series The Tudors.

Bryan has presented Knock Knock and Umbrella for BBC Television, Saturday Night Live for RTE and for three years his live chat show Encore for RTE television in Ireland. He has appeared in many television commercials and has been the voice for a number of advertising campaigns. In the United States his face is well known for the Irish Spring and Pioneer Press TV commercials. His films include Here Are Ladies, A Portrait of the Artist as a Young Man, Solo Shuttle, Mrs. Santa Claus, Sparrow's Trap and Breakpoint and Boy Eats Girl.

Robert Massey Author

Robert was born and raised in Dublin. He graduated Commerce in UCD and completed his postgraduate in Marketing at the Smurfit School of Business, Blackrock. His first play Deadline was developed as part of the Playtalk programme at the Abbey Theatre and produced by Lane Productions at Andrews Lane Studio in February 2006, transferring to Andrews Lane Theatre in April of that year. His second play Over and Out was also produced by Lane Productions, opening at the Civic Theatre Tallaght in May 2008 before embarking on a nation-wide tour of nine venues including Draoícht in Blanchardstown and the Cork Opera House. He lives in Clane, Co Kildare with his wife Kathleen and their daughters Ella and Robyn.

Jim Culleton Director

Jim Culleton is the Artistic Director of Fishamble for which he most recently directed The Pride of Parnell Street by Sebastian Barry (on tour nationally and to London, France, Germany and the US), Noah and the Tower Flower by Sean McLoughlin (winner of the Stewart Parker Trust Award and The Irish Times Best New Play Award), Forgotten by Pat Kinevane (on tour nationally and to Paris, Prague, Sibiu and Edinburgh), short plays for Whereabouts (winner of The Irish Times Special Judges' Award) and Monged by Gary Duggan (winner of the Stewart Parker Trust Award, on tour nationally, to the UK and as a staged reading in New York).

He has also directed for Amnesty International, Pigsback, 7:84 (Scotland), Project Arts Centre, Amharclann de hlde, Tinderbox, The Passion Machine, The Ark, Second Age, RTE Radio 1, The Belgrade, The Abbey/Peacock, Semper Fi, TNL Canada, Scotland's Ensemble @ Dundee Rep, Draíocht, Barnstorm, TCD School of Drama, Origin (New York) and RTE lyric fm. His productions have won or been nominated for awards, including The Irish Times Theatre Awards, Entertainment & Media Awards, In Dublin Theatre Awards and TMA Awards, and he was recently shortlisted for an Allianz Business to Arts Award. He has edited and contributed to books for New Island, Carysfort Press, Ubu, Amnesty International, European Theatre Convention and NCI.

Blaithin Sheerin
Set and Costume Designer

Blaithin trained at NCAD and and Motley Theatre Design Course, London. Previous designs for Fishamble include From Both Hips and True Believers. Designs at the Abbey and Peacock include The Dandy Dolls/Riders to the Sea/Purgatory, Portia Coughlan, Drama at Inish, Bailegangaire, The Sanctuary Lamp, The Morning After Optimism, Made in China, As the Beast Sleeps, Eden, Savoy, The Drawer Boy, and On Such As We. Designs for Rough Magic include Olga, Midden, The Whisperers, The School for Scandal, Northern Star and Digging for Fire. For the Gate Theatre Blaithin has designed the core set for the Beckett Festival in New York, Aristocrats and You Never Can Tell. Other design includes The Comedy of Errors (RSC), The Importance of Being Earnest (The Yorkshire Playhouse), Our Father (Almeida Theatre), Honour (b*spoke theatre), The Cavalcaders and Juno and the Paycock (Lyric Theatre). She has also worked with Druid, Charabanc, Prime Cut and Galloglass.

Mark Galione Lighting Designer

In Ireland, Mark's lighting designs include work for The Peacock, The Civic, Classic Stage Ireland, Fishamble, Barabbas, Guna Nua, Cois Ceim, Hands Turn, Mask, Vesuvius, Dance Theatre of Ireland, Irish Modern Dance Theatre, High Resolution Lighting, Production Services Ireland, The Waterfront, The Ark and Calipo. In Britain, he has designed for Nigel Charnock, Gaby Agis, Sadler's Wells, The Royal Ballet, Ricochet, Small Axe, Soho Theatre Co, The Sherman Theatre and Emilyn Claid. For Fishamble, Mark has lit *The Y2K Festival, Still, Shorts, Tadhg Stray Wandered In, Pilgrims In The Park, Monged* and *Noah and the Tower Flower*.

Ivan Birthistle and Vincent Doherty
Sound Designers/Composers

Vincent and Ivan decided to pool their talents a few years ago and now work on an ongoing collaborative basis.

Past work includes: *Noah and the Tower Flower, The Gist of It, Monged* and *Tadgh Stray Wandered In* (Fishamble); *The Playboy of the Western World, Saved, The Alice Trilogy* and *True West* (The Abbey); *Pentecost* (Rough Magic); *Miss Julie* and *Blackbird* (Landmark); *Roberto Zucco, This is Not a Life, Beckett's Ghosts, Shooting Gallery, Far Away* and *The Massacre @ Paris* (Bedrock); *Fewer Emergencies* (Randolf S.D); *The Sanctuary Lamp* and *Honour* (B'spoke); *God's Grace, Adrenalin* and *Slaughter* (Semper-Fi); *Dancing at Lughnasa, Much Ado About Nothing, Shadow of a Gunman* and *True West* (The Lyric); *The Dilemma of a Ghost, The Kings of the Kilburn High Road, Once Upon a Time* and *Not So Long Ago* (Arambe); *Does She Take Sugar* (Jean Butler and the Project Arts Centre); *Luca* (Barrabas); *Hollow Ground* and *Liberty West* (Coisceim); *All About Town* and W*underkind* (Calipo); *An Image of the Rose* (Whiplash); *No Messin' With The Monkeys* (The Ark) and *Feint* (Pan Pan).

Other sound designs include:

For Vincent: *Mud, Foley* and *Lolita* (The Corn Exchange); *Blasted* and *Night Just Before the Forest* (Bedrock); *Three Days of Rain* (Rough Magic); *Still* (Fishamble); *What the Dead Want, The Mai* and *Within 24 Hours of Dance* (Semper-Fi).

For Ivan: *Ladies and Gents; Ten; Butterflies; Breakfast With Versace; Within 24 Hours of Dance* and *The White Piece* (I.M.D.T).

Orla Flanagan Producer

Orla has recently returned to Fishamble in the role of General Manager following the completion of a fellowship in arts management at the John F. Kennedy Centre for the Performing Arts in Washington D.C., a ten month programme, for which she was awarded the *Diageo Sponsored Fulbright Award for the Performing and Visual Arts*. She previously produced Fishamble's productions of *Noah and the Tower Flower* by Sean McLoughlin, *The Gist of It* by Rodney Lee, *Forgotten* by Pat Kinevane, a revival tour of *Monged* by Gary Duggan and the site-specific, multi-writer production of *Whereabouts (The Irish Times* Theatre Award winner 2006). Prior to this, she was the Literary Officer at the Abbey Theatre since 2001. She has also worked as Marketing Administrator at the National Concert Hall and has produced a number of shows for the Dublin Fringe Festival. In 2005, she worked as a trainee dramaturg at the Sundance Theatre Lab, Utah, and the Schaubuhne's Festival of International New Drama 05, Berlin.

Highlight Productions
Marketing and Publicity

Highlight Productions was established in March 2008 by Marie Rooney as an independent production, marketing and arts management company. Since then, Highlight Productions has been providing a range of services to several clients including Irish Theatre Institute and Dublin Fringe Festival. Most recently, Highlight was responsible for the marketing of b*spoke Theatre Company's production of *The Sanctuary Lamp*, written and directed by Tom Murphy. She is delighted to be working with

Fishamble: The New Play Company.
Rooney has a wealth of experience in all areas of theatre. She was previously Deputy Director of the Gate Theatre for many years. Highlight Productions has a number of new projects in development, with productions and co-productions planned into 2010

Gavin Kostick Literary Officer

Gavin is the Literary Officer for Fishamble. He works with new writers for theatre through script development, readings and a variety of courses. Gavin is also an award-winning playwright. He has written over a dozen plays which have been produced in Dublin, on tour around Ireland, the UK, New York, Philadelphia and Romania. He is currently working on new plays for Fishamble, Kabosh and Whiplash, and an Opera with composer Raymond Deane for RTE Lyric. As a performer he gained *The Spirit of the Fringe Award* 2007 for his production of *Joseph Conrad's Heart of Darkness: Complete* which he is taking to the Dublin Theatre Festival in 2008

Marketa Puzman Stage Director

Marketa has ten years experience of working in film and TV, both in the Art and Production Departments, in the Czech Republic. During her time in the film business, Marketa worked on 17 feature films - credits include *Hart's War, Les Misérables, Last Holiday, Van Helsing* and many television projects including BBC's *The Scarlet Pimpernel* series. Since relocating from Prague to Dublin, Marketa has worked in performing arts management, initially in contemporary dance as General Manager with Dance Theatre of Ireland, until she joined Fishamble, for which she produced *The Pride of Parnell Street,* a revival tour of *Forgotten* and a reading of *My Name Is Rachel Corrie* in association with Amnesty International.

Des Kenny Production Manager

Credits include *The Pride of Parnell Street, Noah & the Tower Flower, Pilgrims in the Park, Tadhg Stray Wandered In, The Gist of It* and *Monged* for Fishamble, *Far Away, Urban Ghosts* and *Shooting Gallery* for Bedrock, *Alone It Stands* for Lane Productions and Yew Tree Theatre Company, *Triple Espresso* for Lane Productions, *Dublin by Lamplight, Mud* and *Everyday* for The Corn Exchange, *Sleeping Beauty* for Landmark/Helix and *How Many Miles to Babylon, Macbeth* and *Othello* for Second Age.

Clive Welsh Stage Manager

Work at the Abbey Theatre includes *A Number, Saved, Terminus, Woman and Scarecrow* and *The Recruiting Officer.* Other work includes *King Ubu* at Galway Arts Festival (Finewine), *Macbeth* (Siren), *Under Ice* at the Edinburgh Fringe Festival (RAW), *Intimate Details* with CoisCeim Dance Theatre for the Ryder Cup Opening Ceremony (Longroad & CoisCeim), *A Streetcar Named Desire* (Opera Ireland), *The Pearl Fishers* at the Gaiety Theatre (Anna Livia), *The Nutcracker* (Irish Youth Ballet), *Further Than The Furthest Thing* (HATCH Theatre Company & Project Arts Centre) and St Patrick's Festival Dublin.

RANK

Robert Massey

Characters

CARL CONWAY, *thirty-two, a taxi driver*
GEORGE KELLY, *fifty-seven, a taxi driver*
'TWO IN THE BUSH', *twenty-nine, a taxi driver*
JACK 'JACKIE' FARRELL, *fifty-four, a casino owner*
FRED FARRELL, *thirty, his son*

This play is set in the Great Dublin Area, Ireland

This text went to press before the end of rehearsals and so may differ slightly from the play as performed.

ACT ONE

Scene One

JACKIE, FRED *and* CARL *are sitting in* JACKIE*'s house.* JACKIE *and* FRED *are eating,* CARL *is not.* JACKIE *is a well-put-together man in his fifties, who, in his own mind, dresses like he is in his thirties.* FRED *is a bodybuilder with a shaved head and an unnatural tan. There is a cordless phone on the table which* FRED *is very aware of – he is awaiting a call.* CARL *is overweight and he's drinking a cup of tea.*

JACKIE. …So bearing all of that in mind I want you to listen carefully.

CARL. I am. I'm listening.

JACKIE. Because there is a lesson in this for you. It has a whatyoucallit?

FRED. A moral.

JACKIE. Wonders will never cease – Well done, son.

FRED. Thanks, Dad.

JACKIE. It has a moral – for you.

CARL. Is this about my weight again?

JACKIE. No.

CARL. Because…

JACKIE. It's not about your weight.

CARL. Okay.

JACKIE. But you do need to do something about that.

CARL. I know I do.

FRED. You're after piling on more since I saw you last and that's only a couple of weeks now.

JACKIE (*re:* FRED). He's sitting in with us in case I need him.

CARL. Rightio.

FRED. Just not a healthy state for you to be in, Carl.

CARL. It's difficult for me.

FRED. How is it?

CARL. Well…

FRED. How?

CARL. Well, it was fine when I was teaching, I was always on my feet, but…

FRED. What?

CARL. But these past two years I'm just stuck driving that taxi. I'm not getting a chance to do any exercise and…

FRED. No.

CARL. No?

FRED. It's more than that.

JACKIE. It's your diet.

FRED. It's the fucking food you're eating, Carl.

JACKIE. You look at Freddie here.

FRED. Take a look.

JACKIE. He's in peak condition now.

FRED (*demonstrating*). You see?

JACKIE. And he sits on his arse day and night.

FRED. Who does?

JACKIE. You do.

FRED. I work hard.

JACKIE. Alright.

FRED. That club doesn't run itself, does it?

JACKIE. No, your wife runs it.

FRED. Jasmine's the assistant manager, Carl.

JACKIE. She hires, fires, does the roster, lodges the money, so – what exactly is left?

FRED. Troubleshooting.

JACKIE. I don't know. Maybe it's just me.

CARL. And all your other stuff, of course.

JACKIE. What other stuff?

CARL. Nothing. Just all your other…

FRED. Be careful now, Carl.

JACKIE. You've been listening to your father-in-law again.

FRED. Here we go.

JACKIE. What did I tell you about that?

CARL. You told me not to.

JACKIE. I told you George Kelly is chock-full of fucking shit.

Especially when he takes to talking about me and mine.

CARL. He never talks about you at all, Jackie.

JACKIE. And you can fucking tell George Kelly I said that when you see him next.

CARL. He doesn't even know I know you.

JACKIE. Tell him get down off his little pedestal and watch his mouth before he comes to open it.

CARL. Rightio.

JACKIE. And then you knock it on the head with the Big Macs before your fucking heart gives out.

Pause.

CARL. I don't eat Big Macs.

JACKIE. Whatever then.

Pause.

CARL. I don't eat meat, full stop.

FRED. Fuck off.

CARL. Honestly I don't.

JACKIE. Don't try to take the piss now. I'm not in the humour today.

CARL. Seriously, Jackie. Never have.

JACKIE. How long do I know you, Carl?

CARL. I don't know.

JACKIE. How long?

CARL. Well, it's…

JACKIE. How long?

CARL. Couple of years.

JACKIE. More like three.

CARL. Is it?

JACKIE. It is.

FRED. At least.

CARL. Okay.

JACKIE. Now that's a long time, Carl.

CARL. I suppose.

JACKIE. No suppose about it.

FRED. It is what it is.

JACKIE. A long fucking time.

CARL. It is then.

JACKIE. And only today I find out.

CARL. What?

JACKIE. You're a vegetarian.

CARL. Well, I…

JACKIE. Because that's the kind of thing I think I should know about.

CARL (*unsure where this is going*). Yeah?

JACKIE. Especially with anyone I'm allowing this type of credit to.

CARL. I'm not following.

JACKIE. Because now I'm thinking – what else are you hiding on me?

CARL. Nothing, Jackie. I'm always straight with you. You know that.

JACKIE. Do I really?

CARL. I'm here every week with your money, amn't I?

JACKIE. Are you trying to be fucking funny with me now, Carl?

CARL. Alright, I know lately…

JACKIE. Lately, yes lately. Lately you're short. Way short and please don't play this like we haven't discussed it till I'm blue in the fucking face.

CARL. I'm not. I'm fully aware that the last few weeks…

JACKIE. Months now.

CARL. The last couple of months I've let it all get a bit out of control, yes.

FRED. You've lost the run of yourself altogether, Carl. What were you thinking Monday night?

CARL. I was this close to breaking even.

FRED. I'm surprised you were let out the front door.

JACKIE. I'm getting soft in my old age.

FRED. You must be.

JACKIE. It stops today. Now I've warned you several times.

FRED. So you've had your warnings, Carl.

JACKIE. Today is most definitely your day. Be under no illusion. All this with you is coming to a head…

FRED. Today.

CARL. I am going to get a grip on it. Starting this week. I'm going to be brand new from here on in, Jackie.

JACKIE. See, I'd really like to believe you with that. Really I would, but…

CARL. Why won't you?

JACKIE. I just don't feel like I know you any more.

CARL. Jesus, Jackie – it never came up.

JACKIE. 'Never came up.' Every fucking week you're sitting there and I'm banging on at you about the state you're in.

CARL. Same as everyone else is.

FRED. And you're a vegetarian.

CARL. I don't call myself that.

JACKIE. Well, it has to be asked, Carl. How many vegetables can one man eat?

CARL. I don't eat vegetables at all.

FRED. Ahh, for fuck's sake.

JACKIE. I know you don't. Vegetables are not your problem. It's the lack of them that is. It's the doughnuts. It's the Cheese and Onion. It's the fucking Mars Bars, Carl.

CARL. And I'm going to do something about it now.

FRED. With all your education, Carl – It's a disgrace, really.

JACKIE. A total disgrace. Nothing short of.

CARL. I was thinking I might go down to the Weight Watchers.

JACKIE. And there's no excuse because we all know this is not your natural state. This is a result of pure gluttony – there wasn't a fucking pick on you until after your wife went and died – and that's barely a year ago now.

CARL. They've these classes every Tuesday evening…

JACKIE. And I couldn't give two fucks what you look like, you understand. That's all your own business as far as I'm concerned.

CARL. In the community centre…

JACKIE. But with all that weight and the amount of stress you've brought on yourself with these activities you insist on engaging in – I'm worried about you making it to the end of today without keeling over.

CARL. Nice to know you care.

JACKIE. Well, caring costs me fuck-all.

The phone rings. FRED *looks at* JACKIE.

What are you looking at me for?

FRED. I better take this.

JACKIE. I know you had.

FRED. It's the one I'm waiting on.

JACKIE. I know it is. Go and take it.

FRED. Will you be okay here?

JACKIE. Well, I think I can manage, son.

FRED. Okay, so.

FRED *picks up the phone and leaves.*

CARL. So – (*Taking out an envelope with* JACKIE*'s money.*) Look – Listen – What I wanted to propose to you, Jackie, is that…

JACKIE. I'll tell you the story first.

CARL. Oh yeah.

JACKIE. Before we get into what I'm pretty sure we're getting into, because I think this might be the last option I have. To try and actually get through to you without…

He places his blue bat on the table.

CARL. It's going to be alright, Jackie.

JACKIE. *Good.* So I have my fingers in a few pies. Some hot, some cold. The point being I have a wide range of interests.

CARL. A portfolio.

JACKIE. So to speak. I can't be relying on fuckers like you paying what they owe me to feed my family, now, can I?

CARL. Of course you can.

JACKIE. So I always keep myself a varied and strong spread of income streams. The casino, the club, the limos, the couriers. Bits and bobs, but – let's be perfectly clear – there are those who believe I'm running a few lines on the wrong side of the law, in the technical sense of that phrase.

CARL. I wouldn't know anything about that.

JACKIE. That's what I'm basically known for – basically. That's what George Kelly fills yours and everyone else's heads full of, isn't it? Jackie Farrell's a common criminal, a fucking toerag – that's it, isn't it?

CARL. Well, I'd never dream of calling you…

JACKIE. And that's just fine with me, Carl. I stopped bothering about that a long time ago. I've come to realise that there is only one basic difference between me and all the George Kellys of this world, and that's fear and shame.

CARL. That's two things, isn't it?

JACKIE. I'll rephrase it then. The fear of shame. The fear of having the police call to your front door because your poor mammy might hear about it and get upset. Of getting your name printed in the papers because your neighbours might read about it and think bad of you. The fear of – and God forbid this as far as Georgie was concerned – of maybe having to go to prison because your father would have no option but to throw himself in the fucking Liffey. You see, none or any of that ever bothered me one jot. I never gave a bollocks. My family deserved the best and I provided it for them. Only a coward wouldn't. And if George had of had

just a little bit of bottle to go with all his brains and personality, we could have been some team together. If he could
have thrown a bit of caution to the never-never when I first
asked him to, right at the start – because look how he ended
up anyway – both his folks, his wife and his only little
daughter gone, well before their time, and him left with not a
pot to piss in. Where's the reward in that for all his 'straight
and narrow'?

What the fuck was I talking about anyway?

CARL. You were telling me the story. The one with the moral.

JACKIE. That's right – my wife thinks I've George Kelly on
the brain my whole life.

CARL. Maybe she's right.

JACKIE. Carmel's right about most things.

CARL. So…

JACKIE. So, a lowlife I may be.

CARL. No you're not.

JACKIE. But here's the funny thing – I happen to have one
little business that is making me more than all those other
ventures combined – and it's completely legit.

CARL. Really?

JACKIE. Really.

CARL. What is it?

JACKIE. It's in the service industry.

CARL. So it's…

JACKIE. A chat line.

CARL. Like a…

JACKIE. Phone sex, you know. Women talking dirty while
fellas whack off.

CARL. Very good.

JACKIE. And very legal. All above board. Registered for VAT and paying tax on the substantial profits.

CARL. Well done.

JACKIE. Yes, it was. Started it up five years ago. Ran it out of the house, hired the line, got two of my nieces to do the talking. Put the ads in the paper – one ninety-nine a minute with a minimum of five minutes – and the fucking floodgates opened. A gold mine. I had to hire an office after six months. Now I have twenty full-time girls on the books and the lines are open round the clock. You want a wank Christmas Day – we're open for business. It is cleaning up and I couldn't be happier.

CARL. That's a great story.

JACKIE. What is?

CARL. That.

JACKIE. How is that the story?

CARL. That's not the story?

JACKIE. What's the fucking moral to that?

CARL. Well, just...

JACKIE. What?

CARL. That – you know – sometimes – you can do just as well – doing things – straight – as you can – by – you know – other means.

JACKIE. And how is that going to help you?

CARL. I don't know. I thought maybe it was one of those... like a riddle, you know.

JACKIE. It's not.

CARL. No, I know.

JACKIE. That's not the story.

CARL. Okay, I see.

JACKIE. That's just the background.

CARL. I misunderstood.

JACKIE. Are you in a rush somewhere, Carl?

CARL. Not at all.

JACKIE. Because – please – don't let me fucking hold you…

CARL. Really… no, I'm here for you…

JACKIE. So I can finish, can I?

CARL. Of course you can – I want to hear it, I do.

JACKIE. You're sure?

CARL. Positive – yes.

Pause.

JACKIE. The best girl I have on the line – nothing short of – is Kylie.

CARL. That her real name?

JACKIE. It conjures an image.

CARL. Rightio.

JACKIE. Now, this girl works her arse off. Puts in the hours. Does a fine thorough job on every call, every day from the first to the last, and that type of positive attitude has got her a lot of regular customers. That's the key to earning. On weekend shifts she can notch up to a grand, and half of that goes to the house – so, needless to say, I was always very happy with her overall performance.

CARL. Sounds like a real asset.

JACKIE. So she comes to me round this time last year and tells me her sister is looking for work. I'm thinking – stroke of luck. Good girls are not easy to come by and I am a firm believer that a work ethic runs in the family. It's taught from a young age. I'm sorry I wasn't around enough to instil it in my own, so as far as I'm concerned the sister is hired. I just need to meet with her. As a formality, you see.

CARL. Straightforward.

JACKIE. So I tell Kylie to bring this girl – Britney – in to me the next morning. She insists on sitting in on the interview. Says her sister can get a bit nervous. What do I care – fine. So they're both there a half hour early – you just can't buy that kind of commitment – and Britney, she's a fine-looking young woman, not that that matters a shit, but I have a good feeling about the whole situation.

CARL. And so you should.

JACKIE. So I say, 'Good morning.' I shake her hand. She gives me a sweet little smile and they both sit down. I kick off with the basics – age, address and so on so forth – and it's Kylie giving me all the answers – you see – Britney is sitting there like a fucking mute and I'm starting to get a bit concerned. She had mentioned the shyness, sure, but I had to hear the girl's voice. That's a prerequisite, you see. I don't give a fuck if you've got no arms or legs – all I need for this is the voice.

CARL. That makes sense.

JACKIE. So I tell her – 'Look,' I say to her – 'Your sister here is my best girl. I am sure you are going to do great. I know you are a bit nervous – but there's no need – you're amongst friends.' I just need to hear her say one line, that's it – and the job's hers. She gives me another nod – you see. Lips still sealed. So I turn my back, close my eyes and I wait for her to say it.

CARL. Say what?

JACKIE. The line.

CARL. What line?

JACKIE. The same line I get all of them to say in every interview.

CARL. Which is?

JACKIE. 'I am going to suck your big cock dry.'

CARL. Rightio.

JACKIE. So I'm standing there, eyes closed, waiting. Ten seconds, thirty, a full minute – not a fucking dicky-bird. And

I can hear Kylie whispering to her – 'Just say it, say the line, go on.' And eventually I hear her start off. And it all becomes clear.

CARL. What?

JACKIE. Britney has a stutter.

CARL. You're joking me.

JACKIE. And it's a really fucking bad one. Worse than any I ever heard. She must have said 'suck' twenty times. No joke. 'I am going to suck… suck… suck… suck… suck…suck… suck…' You get the idea.

CARL. I do.

JACKIE. So I stop her – I can't take it any more. And then Kylie erupts. Apparently I'm supposed to let her finish. It's the height of ignorance to interrupt her…

CARL. Well, that's true actually.

JACKIE. I'm a busy fucking man – and I talk straight to people and I tell her the basic home truths. You cannot talk dirty on a phone sex line for a living when you have a stutter.

CARL. A stammer.

JACKIE. What's that?

CARL. She has a stammer. It's different.

JACKIE. How the fuck is it different?

CARL. It just is – Don't worry about it – it's no big deal.

JACKIE. No, really, I'm intrigued.

CARL. I'm sorry I brought it up.

JACKIE. Well, you did – so you better follow it through. Now what's the fucking difference?

CARL. Well, you said she was repeating the word over and over. 'I am going to suck… suck… suck… suck…' and so on, see – she's stammering the word. It's a stammer. If she had a stutter she would get stuck on the word – 'I am going to sss, I am going to sss, I am going to sss, ssss, ssss…'

JACKIE. Unbelievable.

CARL. Yeah, well…

JACKIE. Truly.

CARL. Sorry… (*Pause.*) I'm still not sure what the moral is…

JACKIE. That's because I'm not finished.

CARL. Rightio.

JACKIE. I was interrupted by your fucking stammering shit.

CARL. I'll keep quiet – what happened?

JACKIE. Well, Kylie's well and truly losing it and Britney is crying her fucking eyes out. I'm unrepentant, you see, because I can't understand what these women want from me. I tell them – for fuck's sake – I'm waiting for Jeremy Beadle to walk in – are they winding me up? Not a bit of it. Kylie tells me I'm a fucking pig – that her sister needs to overcome this impediment and it's discriminating cunts like me that are holding her back. That Kylie girl has quite a mouth on her.

CARL. Works both ways.

JACKIE. That's how you have to look at it. So basically it's coming down to this – either I give her a run or Kylie's leaving. Fucking despicable. Blackmailing me. But what was I supposed to do? I say fine. The world's gone mad but she can start tomorrow. Two of them get up and go – both in for work early the next morning. And Britney takes her first call.

CARL. And…

JACKIE. And within a month she's the highest earner on the line.

CARL. Fuck off.

JACKIE. Turns out they love it. The stuttering.

CARL. Stammering.

JACKIE. Whatever the fuck – It's the kinkiest thing those sick bastards have ever heard. That stammering beaut has more regular customers than all the other girls put together. There is a constant queue to talk to her and every call she does takes at least half an hour because that's how long it takes her to spit the fucking words out.

CARL. Jesus.

JACKIE. So you see the moral, don't you?

CARL. I think so.

JACKIE. Tell me?

CARL. Something about – overcoming odds, you know – rising above your limitations, accepting yourself for who you are – you know, that whole – embracing diversity. There's a place for everybody.

JACKIE. Bollocks.

CARL. Okay.

JACKIE. The moral is that no matter how much you think you know about people – likes, dislikes, what will or won't turn them on or off – at the end of the day, nobody knows nothing about anybody.

CARL. Rightio.

JACKIE. Because I think you think you know me now, Carl.

CARL. What?

JACKIE. I do, and this is the point – I think you think you've figured me out and that somehow you've got my number.

CARL. Not at all, Jack.

JACKIE. You see, I know you, Carl.

CARL *gives a gentle laugh.*

What?

CARL. You just said nobody knows anyone.

JACKIE. I know the fucking kind of you.

CARL. Yeah?

JACKIE. Oh yeah.

CARL. What kind is that then?

JACKIE. The kind of grubby fucker who turns up today still short of what he owes. After being told last week, politely, but in no uncertain terms, *not to*.

CARL. Well, that's what I wanted to talk to you about, isn't it?

JACKIE. There's fuck-all to talk about, Carl. We're here now. At the crunch. So to speak. We have arrived in yes-or-no territory. So, yes or no – Is everything you owe the house in that envelope as we agreed?

CARL. The thing about it is...

JACKIE. Yes or no, Carl. Please don't say anything else.

CARL. No.

JACKIE. Well, it was always going to be a long shot. But I was hopeful, Carl, I have to say.

CARL (*putting the envelope on the table*). There's two grand there. That's double my normal the last few weeks and it's every penny I have because I wanted to show you I'm deadly serious about all of this. I won't be in the club this week.

JACKIE. You won't, no.

CARL. I won't be in there any more – I can't be. I'm out, you see.

JACKIE. You're out?

CARL. Of all of it. I have to be. It's time for a change now. I'm going to focus and work my arse off. I understand my responsibilities. Loud and clear since last week, don't you worry. I'll be in that taxi twenty hours a day, every day. And I'll bring you another two next Wednesday...

JACKIE. You owe five.

CARL. Please – hear me out, Jackie – I'm being straight with you now. This is it. This is all I can do. Two is all I can manage in the week. Then the week after that I'll give you the last bit and that's me. I'm finished with all this bullshit.

JACKIE. Don't try kidding a kidder.

CARL. I'm not kidding. You see – I think I might have a problem.

JACKIE. You *might* have?

CARL. I *could* have, yeah. And I was thinking that I should maybe make contact, you know. With the Gamblers Anonymous crowd.

JACKIE. Mother of Jaysus.

CARL. And then I could go and get myself down to the Weight Watchers too.

JACKIE. I'm looking for Jeremy Beadle again.

CARL. And start to sort it all out, you see. But I need a little bit more time. That's all. Not too much to ask, is it? A fortnight. That's all. Please.

JACKIE (*softly now*). Tragic this, Carl. Nothing short of.

CARL. Please, Jackie.

JACKIE. I was only saying it to Fred this morning – you were one of the best poker players I ever saw sit at a table.

CARL. I was a different man then.

JACKIE. Two, three years ago. The maths teacher sent to give us all a lesson on statistics.

CARL. Yeah.

JACKIE. Carl Conway the Card Counter.

CARL. Different times they were.

JACKIE. And you haven't played a hand for six months at least. What's happened to you, Carl?

CARL. You know what's happened to me, Jackie, for fuck's sake.

JACKIE. All I know is you're spinning your life away like a halfwit on a *roulette wheel*. Fuck-all skill in a roulette wheel.

CARL. Easy to play a machine. You need your nerve for poker.

JACKIE. That you do.

CARL. I can't look people in the eye any more – I'm fucking walking into lamp-posts, no joke. It's the weight maybe.

JACKIE. Maybe.

CARL. I can't seem to get used to myself. Not like I am now.

JACKIE (*taking the envelope*). Okay, Carl.

CARL. Thank you, Jackie. I really appreciate this.

JACKIE. I like these little chats we have, you know.

CARL. Yeah?

JACKIE. Oh yeah. I look forward to them all week.

CARL. I do too.

JACKIE. Like having George Kelly himself sitting back beside me.

CARL. It's not, is it?

JACKIE. So true, what they say.

CARL. What's that?

JACKIE. How a 'daddy's girl' always ends up marrying her father in some form or other.

CARL. You're having me on now.

JACKIE. Oh no, Carl – if only you fucking knew. You and Georgie are turning out to be two peas in the proverbial in every way going.

CARL. I'll tell him you said that. He'll get a laugh out of it anyway.

JACKIE. No he won't. Not in the slightest.

CARL. Rightio.

JACKIE. But it is good for me to have someone intelligent to talk to again after such a long time.

CARL. I'm glad you feel that way, Jackie.

JACKIE. Someone I can have a proper conversation with, regarding subjects that are relevant to people who consider things. I find that very stimulating.

CARL. My thoughts exactly.

Across the table, JACKIE *holds both of* CARL*'s hands with his and then kicks* CARL *very hard in the shin.*

(*Shouts.*) Fuck.

JACKIE *keeps hold of* CARL*'s hands and leans in towards him, touching forehead to forehead.*

JACKIE. Easy. Easy now. Shhhhh. Let's not disturb herself.

CARL. Oh, fuck's sake, Jackie.

JACKIE. I know. I know. Nothing worse than a kick in the shin. I still remember that from school days. A kick in the bollocks you could deal with. Truth be told – there was some strange pleasure to be had from a good kick in the nuts. But a toecap straight in the shin. Now that's pure fucking pain.

CARL (*in agony*). Jesus Christ.

JACKIE (*holding* CARL*'s face now*). Listen to me carefully now.

CARL. Please…

JACKIE. You were told, Carl. You were told how this works. It doesn't change because you ask it to.

CARL. But I thought we were…

JACKIE (*face to face, intimate*). What? What did you think?

CARL. That we were…

JACKIE. Friends?

CARL. I just…

JACKIE. Children have friends, Carl. Fourteen-year-old boys have friends. We're grown men. There's your family – there's your work – and that's that.

CARL. This shouldn't be happening to me, Jackie. None of this should be happening to me.

JACKIE (*standing up*). On your feet now, son. Let's take this out the back.

CARL. Jackie, please, no. For Christ's sake.

JACKIE (*leaning over, into his ear*). You're leaving this house with a hiding, Carl. For all the world to see and know. Then you're bringing me back everything you owe before this day is out or you're a fucking dead man. Nothing short of. We'll make up next week, or maybe we won't. I never gave a shite about those things – this is what it is – now up on your feet.

CARL. Ahhh, what am I after doing?

JACKIE. Let's go.

CARL. Look how I'm after ending myself up.

JACKIE. Quicker the better, Carl, come on.

CARL. What's Jenny going to think of me now?

JACKIE. Nothing – she's dead – now let's go.

CARL. No –

CARL *grabs the table. He is too heavy for* JACKIE *to move – he doesn't even try.*

JACKIE. *Freddie.*

CARL. Jackie, please.

JACKIE. *Fred.*

FRED *enters.*

Grab hold.

FRED. What?

JACKIE. It's time.

FRED (*indicating the phone*). Dad, listen – we have a situation here.

JACKIE. Not with…?

FRED. Yeah.

JACKIE. Is it bad?

FRED. You could say that.

JACKIE (*goes to him*). For fuck's sake, Fred, what are you after doing to me?

FRED. It's not my fault.

JACKIE. It never is, is it? (*To* CARL, *without looking at him.*) Right, scram.

CARL. Really?

JACKIE. Yeah – fuck off. Consider this your lucky day.

CARL. Rightio.

JACKIE. You've got till midnight tonight. Don't make me come looking for it.

CARL. I won't.

JACKIE. Before midnight.

CARL (*on his way out*). Absolutely.

JACKIE. Or Fred'll turn you into a fucking pumpkin. Nothing short of.

FRED. Take it easy, Carl.

JACKIE. *Fred*.

CARL. I'll see you later, Freddie.

CARL *is gone*.

JACKIE. What's happened?

FRED. Calm down now.

JACKIE. I warned you, you wouldn't listen. Go for experience on this. But there is no talking to you, is there?

FRED. I planned it well.

JACKIE. So how are they caught?

FRED. They're not caught – they're back in Kimmage already.

JACKIE. What's the problem then?

FRED. It's what they've left behind them. We have to go back.

Blackout.

Scene Two

The taxi rank at Dublin Airport. GEORGE *and* BUSH *are talking.*

GEORGE. So I leapt out the car, I had to. I ran right in – ran right up to his spotty little face. And I asked him – calmly, mind – what did he think he was playing at? He sees me there. He knows I'm waiting for him. He knows.

So what was his fucking problem?

BUSH. And?

GEORGE. And he tells me – it's the new policy, Bush.

BUSH. Whose new policy?

GEORGE. The manager's. The new owner's. (*With great contempt.*) Esso.

BUSH. What's the new policy?

GEORGE. Self-service.

BUSH. I see.

GEORGE. Now, you know how I feel about self-service, Bush.

BUSH. I know how you feel, George, but it's just the way...

GEORGE. Self-service can ask my bollocks.

BUSH. Yes it can.

GEORGE. Because I have to provide a service, Bush. To every pox-bottle that gets in my taxi. I don't give them the keys, tell them to drive themselves, while I sit in the back and scratch meself, do I?

BUSH. No, you don't.

GEORGE. While I sit in the back and read a paper, do I?

BUSH. No.

GEORGE. It was the only one left, Bush. The only garage in this entire shithole of a cesspool that sent someone out to pump your diesel for you. So you didn't get it on your hands and stink for your whole shift. So you didn't get your trousers soaked if it was raining. So you didn't catch your death of cold in the winter.

BUSH. I know, I know it was.

GEORGE. So I asked to see the manager.

BUSH. You didn't, George, please, tell me you didn't.

GEORGE. I was calm – I was so beyond livid that I was actually very calm. And I told him my side. Calmly.

I told him I was a regular customer for the last thirty years. That I filled up twice a week there. Eighty euro each fill. That's a hundred and sixty euro a week. Fifty-two weeks a year – because you know I don't take holidays.

BUSH. I know.

GEORGE. That's over eight-grand worth of business a year.

BUSH. Jesus, when you put it that way.

GEORGE. What other way is there to put it?

BUSH. Not a one.

GEORGE. And I didn't want much. I told him. All I was asking was for the status quo to remain. The small service of having the youngfella pump my diesel for me.

BUSH. Well done, George. Well done. That's the way to talk to people, you see. I bet you got a result.

GEORGE. I got barred.

BUSH. You got what?

GEORGE. He barred me.

BUSH. He fucking barred you?

GEORGE. Well, not at first. First he told me that the company policy could not be changed for one customer. That in a full week I was the only complaint he had had. That if I didn't like it I should really shop around. He said it was a 'free market'.

BUSH. Well, that's not barring you.

GEORGE. No, he barred me after I finished calling him a cross-born, pox-riddled, son of a whooer's boot.

BUSH. That'll do it.

GEORGE. So I've decided I'm going to burn it down.

BUSH. You can't burn down a petrol station, George. It's full of petrol. You'd blow up the whole village.

GEORGE. Oh, fuck the whole village, Bush. Fuck it. I'd love to see it burn. They're all as bad as each other. The pub I drink in. The shop I buy my groceries. The chipper, the Chinese, Four-Star fucking Pizza.

There's not one of them gives a toss. Whether you go there or not. Whether they ever see you or not. They couldn't care less. And that's a new thing, Bush. You have to believe me. You're a young man. I know.

There was a time when you counted. When people appreciated you, appreciated your trade. Welcomed you, you know?

There was a time when a petrol station would have gone out of their way to get a taxi man's business. Eight grand a year for fuck's sake. They used to give us free car washes, free papers in the evening. They used to make us feel valued, you know. Feel important, like we mattered.

And they used to pump our diesel.

What happened to us, Bush? All of a sudden we're worth fuck-all. Nothing to nobody. What happened?

BUSH. It's not just us, George. It's the whole city now, the whole country.

GEORGE. It is, I know that.

BUSH. It's changed.

GEORGE. It has, that's what I'm saying to you.

BUSH. There's no room for manners any more. People don't have time for them.

GEORGE. They've no time for anything.

BUSH. Or anybody.

GEORGE. And that's right, is it?

BUSH. No, but it is what it is and you need to accept it and learn to live with the fact. Move on and feel a bit better about things.

Look – every fucker out there bar none is out to get us in some way or other, yes, but you shouldn't let that get to you so much. I keep telling you. Try and keep some sort of lid on it. Everyone round here is scared shitless of you at this stage. You're up to ninety, twenty-four-seven and that can't be a good way to be for the old ticker.

GEORGE. If only, though. If only a few more people had complained. At the Esso. Complained about the change. Instead of just accepting everything these pricks decide to do to us. Then they would have had to listen. If only I wasn't on my own all the time.

BUSH. You're not on your own, George.

GEORGE. That's exactly what I am now, Bush.

BUSH. You've always got me.

GEORGE. Are you trying to make me feel better or worse?

BUSH. And Carl, of course.

GEORGE. Another fucking consequence. Haven't heard sight nor light from the little bollix since last week.

BUSH. Me neither.

GEORGE. Whatever's going on with him?

BUSH. I'd say he's just too busy stuffing his face.

Pause.

GEORGE. I'd leave the Aldi alone.

BUSH. The what's that?

GEORGE. The Aldi. I wouldn't burn that down.

BUSH. Very decent of you, George.

GEORGE. They're no better than the rest when it comes down to basic common courtesy – but the prices are great.

BUSH. So I've heard.

GEORGE. I sorted out my toilet rolls there.

BUSH. Well done.

GEORGE. They'd a sale on last week. Pack of sixteen rolls for a fiver. Good quality.

BUSH. Good price.

GEORGE. I'm using between two and three rolls a month, so I reckon two packs will last me a year, no bother.

BUSH. You bought two packs then.

GEORGE. I bought twenty-six. A hundred and thirty euro.

BUSH. I'm afraid to ask – why twenty-six?

GEORGE. 'Cause I reckon that's me done, you see. With toilet rolls.

BUSH. You what?

GEORGE. Well, I'm fifty-seven now. I won't see past seventy. Not with this heart and the family history. My aul' fella didn't get out of his sixties. None of his brothers either. I've another thirteen years tops and even that'll be a miracle.

BUSH. You're after buying your lifetime's supply of toilet rolls.

GEORGE. I'd rather have as much sorted as possible. For the run-in. Then I can relax and just do the time.

BUSH. For fuck's sake.

CARL *enters limping – striving for normality.*

GEORGE. Where the fuck have you been? You don't answer your phone?

CARL. Howya, George. Bush.

GEORGE. You don't answer your door?

CARL. I'm grand, I'm grand.

GEORGE. I was about to call the police. What is going on with you?

CARL. Don't be worrying yourself about me.

BUSH. Are you limping?

CARL. No I'm not.

GEORGE. You are – you're limping.

CARL. I'm just a bit stiff is all.

BUSH. From what?

CARL. I've been doing some exercise.

GEORGE. Well, that's one positive.

BUSH. At least.

GEORGE. Because you really need to start looking after yourself, Carl.

CARL. Don't start on that now.

GEORGE. You really do.

CARL. George.

BUSH. Just stop with all the fucking eating, for Jaysus' sake.

CARL. I told you before – it's glands.

BUSH. Well, stop eating them then.

CARL. Jesus.

BUSH. You're going to end up with all sorts of problems if you keep this shit up.

CARL. Let's not have Doctor Bush. Not today.

BUSH. Diabetes, heart palpitations, erectile dysfunction.

CARL. Alright.

BUSH. Not that that would bother you at all because no self-respecting female is ever going to go near you in that state.

CARL. Enough please.

BUSH. You'll wind up in *The Guinness Book of Records* before the year's out.

CARL. I'm not that fucking big.

BUSH. No – but you'd have to be in the running for the world's fattest vegetarian.

CARL. I don't call myself that.

Pause.

GEORGE. What is it, Carl?

BUSH. Something is up with you alright – you're very touchy with us today and for no good reason, I might add.

CARL. Nothing's up with me, lads, okay? Just drop it.

GEORGE. Yes it is. I can tell. I can tell for months now.

BUSH. Are you shaking?

CARL. It's just cold is all.

BUSH. No it's not.

CARL. Well, I'm just a bit tired then – please back the fuck off me, will yis.

GEORGE. Go home to bed, Carl.

CARL. I wish I could. Look, lads – I need to work. I need to earn.

GEORGE. Here. (*Hands him some money.*) There's a tonne. Off with you. Go on. Get some sleep. And ring me when you get up – I want to talk to you.

CARL. No, George. Not an option. Thanks anyway. I need to stay out. I need to.

GEORGE. Alright, but mind yourself, will you.

Pause.

CARL. How long are yis waiting?

BUSH. Two hours.

CARL. You're joking me.

GEORGE. It's criminal. I'm not working this airport after tonight. It's gone to shite.

BUSH. Altogether.

GEORGE. And when I eventually do manage to get up there I bet you any money I get Swords.

BUSH. Well, if you do, tell the fuckers to get out and walk.

GEORGE. How can I?

BUSH. You take their cases out of the boot, drag them out of the car and tell them to fucking walk.

GEORGE. That's great advice, Bush. Thanks.

CARL. Two hours?

GEORGE. I can't ever remember it as slow as this.

BUSH. They're not calling us up until the buses are filled.

GEORGE. I'm beginning to think he's right, you know.

BUSH. I'm fucking dead right. Those 'green caps' are up there telling everyone there's no taxis. And we're all down here like gobshites waiting. They're on a backhander to fill the buses, George. Why else has it slowed down? Do you think less people are using Dublin Airport?

GEORGE. Do I fuck.

BUSH. Exactly.

GEORGE. Recession, me arse – still three, four holidays a year.

BUSH. So why aren't we flying along?

GEORGE. It's the deregulation, isn't it? Every fucker in town deciding overnight to drive a taxi for a living. No offence, Carl.

CARL. Two fucking hours?

GEORGE. Just means less work to go round now.

BUSH. There's the same amount as always in the kesh here. The queue to get in has gone ridiculous, yes. That's the deregulation, yes – But once you're in here it's still the same twelve rows of ten cars out there. And it's crawling along.

GEORGE. I'm saying it to them when I get up there.

CARL (*panicking*). I can't wait here two hours. I don't have that kind of time to waste. What the fuck am I going to do?

CARL *goes to leave*.

GEORGE. Relax, will you. Come here to me. Look at me. What is it, son? Seriously now. What?

Pause.

CARL. I am in a small bit of hassle, George.

GEORGE. Alright. With what?

CARL. You know Jackie Farrell, don't you?

Pause.

GEORGE. *The* Jackie Farrell?

CARL. Yeah.

GEORGE. My Jackie Farrell?

CARL. Yes.

GEORGE. What about him?

CARL. I've just been over at his house.

GEORGE. And what in the name of Jaysus were you doing there?

CARL. Trying to settle my debts.

GEORGE. You're winding me up now. Please tell me you are.

CARL. I wish I was – I really do. I've had a small run of bad luck these past few months.

GEORGE (*with horror*). Gambling?

CARL. A little bit, yeah.

GEORGE. With Jackie Farrell?

CARL. In one of his clubs.

GEORGE. Oh, Carl.

CARL. Look – don't go making a whole big deal out of it, George, okay –

GEORGE. I don't fucking believe this is happening now.

CARL. I've just let a small bit of shit get on top of me.

GEORGE. Jesus Christ.

BUSH. Calm down, George.

GEORGE. How long have you been at this, Carl?

CARL. I don't know –

GEORGE. *How long?*

BUSH. You'll give yourself that heart attack.

GEORGE. Stay out of it, Bush.

CARL. A year or two, okay?

GEORGE. Fuck.

CARL. Back when Jenny got sick first – it was a small bit of a release for me and…

GEORGE. Oh, so this is my daughter's fault then, is it?

CARL. Of course it's not. Listen to me…

GEORGE. Did she know about it? Before she died – did she know what you were up to?

CARL. I wasn't up to anything. I was just playing a few competitions back then. Pubs and the like. Texas Hold'em, you know – where they deal you two cards face down and you…

GEORGE. I know what Texas fucking Hold'em is, Carl.

CARL. Well, I was good at it, George. I was very good. I won a shitload of prizes at those competitions.

And then I started winning a shitload of cash in casinos.

GEORGE. But all of your winning soon stopped – didn't it?

CARL. I don't really know why –

GEORGE. Because it always does, Carl. That's how it works.

CARL. The last few months I started playing the house. Spinning the wheel. Throwing the dice. And I'll admit – I've gotten myself a bit into the red with it all.

GEORGE. I'll bet he's loving this now. I'll bet he's engineered it on me.

CARL. Who?

GEORGE. What sort of trouble are you in, Carl? How bad is it after getting on you?

CARL. Nothing I can't handle overall. It's just this one little issue I have going on with Jackie.

GEORGE. Oh, that's all it is – is it?

CARL. That's all – yes – and I need to sort it out fairly lively.

BUSH. How much do you owe him?

CARL. Look –

GEORGE. No – answer the man – How much?

CARL. Three grand, okay?

BUSH (*taken aback*). Three fucking grand?

CARL. And he wants it tonight. So that's the position I've found myself in, lads.

BUSH. What happens you can't pay him?

CARL. He's threatening to break me up.

GEORGE. That's not a threat, Carl. That's a statement of fact from that vicious prick.

CARL. I know it is, so…

GEORGE. So what else do you owe?

CARL. Nothing.

GEORGE. Carl.

CARL. Nothing serious, alright?

GEORGE. What else?

CARL. Jesus Christ, George – bits and pieces – okay. No other casinos – just some…

GEORGE. Just some fucking what – and start telling the truth, will you? That's the first step.

CARL. I have credit cards.

GEORGE. More than one?

CARL. Three of them.

GEORGE. How much is on them?

CARL. I don't know, around…

GEORGE. How much?

CARL. Four – maybe five grand.

BUSH. Five fucking grand?

CARL. Roughly speaking…

GEORGE. Between the three or on each?

CARL. On each.

BUSH. Fifteen fucking grand?

CARL. That sort of general region anyway.

GEORGE. And what else?

CARL. Ahh, George.

GEORGE. What else?

CARL. I've a loan out from the credit union.

GEORGE. For…?

CARL. Another five.

BUSH. Twenty fucking grand?

GEORGE. And…? (*Pause*.) And…?

CARL. And I've been missing a few payments on the mortgage.

BUSH. But that should all be clear now, shouldn't it? Insurance with your Jenny?

CARL. We bought it in my name.

BUSH. Shite.

CARL. Yeah.

GEORGE. What are your arrears up to?

CARL. Just over ten at this stage.

BUSH. That's thirty fucking grand there, Carl.

GEORGE. And your three to Jack Farrell.

BUSH. Unreal.

GEORGE. And you haven't a shilling of any of your money left to pay a sinner, have you?

CARL. No, I haven't.

GEORGE. Still think it's not that bad?

CARL. Well, when you put it like that.

GEORGE. What other way is there to put it, son?

Pause.

CARL. I can't breathe, lads.

BUSH. The weight has a lot to do with that too.

GEORGE (*angry*). Bush.

BUSH. What? It does. Pressure on the lungs.

GEORGE. I'll pressure your lungs in a minute.

CARL. What am I going to do, George?

GEORGE. Alright. Alright. We'll sort something out.

CARL. But what, though? Because I can't think straight any more. Estate agent says I'll get less for the house than I owe the bank on it, so I'm stuck. Squeezed dry.

GEORGE. It's doable – in the long run – if we can get you through today – Jack Farrell is the priority for now.

CARL. Well, I'm all out of options as far as he's concerned, so anything you can do for me, lads…

BUSH. That's Fred Farrell's aul' fella, though, isn't it? The one who owns Vixens, you know – the lap-dancing place on Leeson Street?

GEORGE. That's him, yeah.

BUSH. Interesting.

CARL. Have you got an idea, Bush?

BUSH. Not as such – but…

GEORGE. Well, spit it out, will you?

BUSH. I might have shagged his wife.

CARL. You what?

BUSH. Few nights back.

GEORGE. Jackie Farrell's wife has Parkinson's. She's in a fucking wheelchair.

BUSH. Not his wife. Give me some credit.

GEORGE. You don't deserve any.

BUSH. Freddie's. The son's. He manages the place.

CARL. Tell me you're winding us up now.

BUSH. No, honestly. I'm a bit of a regular down there, I'm not too proud to say. Freddie started using me to bring the dancers in in the evenings and drop them back home at clocking off. For their own health and safety, he says. Fucking brilliant gig – I'd do it for free if they asked, but they insist on paying their way. Friday night last – I dropped the wife home.

GEORGE. She's a lap dancer?

BUSH. Not at all – she takes the money at the door. Tells the girls where to go. What to do. It's her that runs the place, really, he does fuck-all. He can barely read. Don't ask me how he got her to marry him because I'll tell you what, lads – she's better-looking than any of the ones down there swinging round the poles. You want to see her. A little cracker. Fake tits, fake tan, fake hair, fucking perfect.

CARL. What are you after doing?

BUSH. I've been dying to tell you – so she jumps in the front which they don't normally do, so I'm under pressure from the start.

CARL. For fuck's sake.

BUSH. She gives me the address out in Stillorgan. Flashes me a sweet little smile. And we're off.

GEORGE. We're off alright.

BUSH. I hadn't reached Baggot Street and she's into it. Apparently, her Freddie's no more than a mouth. All talk, no action. Not fulfilling her needs, you see. You with me?

GEORGE. We wish we weren't.

CARL. Go on.

BUSH. I have figured out exactly who she is at this stage of the game and I am making a serious mental note to run as fast as I can from this situation I have brewing, but…

CARL. But?

BUSH. But I have the beginnings of a major horn by the time we're in Donnybrook. By the time we get out to Stillorgan village I could have steered that car with me knob.

CARL. I don't fucking believe this.

BUSH. So we get out to the house. Gorgeous place. Do you know it?

GEORGE. No, I don't.

BUSH. Sort of place I'd really love, you know. With the big garden and the high trees all around it. That cobblelock stuff in the driveway and the lovely patio all round the...

CARL. Would you go on, for fuck's sake.

BUSH. Your man is inside in bed.

GEORGE. Little Freddie's in the house?

BUSH. He's not little any more, George.

CARL. He's the polar opposite of little, is what he is.

BUSH. So she tells me to turn off the lights and drive round the back. She doesn't want to disturb him, you see.

GEORGE. Very thoughtful of her.

BUSH. So there's fourteen on the meter. She gives me twenty. Tells me to keep the change. Thanks very much. And then her hand moves on to the door handle and for just a split second it looks like I am going to get away with it. Then...

CARL. What?

BUSH. Then she looks back over her shoulder at me.

'I got a new tattoo last month.' She says, 'Would you like to see my new tattoo?'

CARL. You're making this up, Bush.

BUSH. As God is my fucking witness. I am on the verge of tears with the restraint at this stage.

'I would, chicken,' I said.

'I have a great interest in art.'

CARL. You didn't say that.

BUSH. Wait till I tell you. Up she gets, on her knees in the front seat. Turns and faces the window. Hikes up the skirt to show me her little blue G-string – and right there in the middle of her left cheek – The Rolling Stones' trademark. You know the thing I'm talking about…

CARL. What thing?

BUSH. I've a picture of it – (*Takes out his phone.*)

GEORGE. You took a picture of her arse.

BUSH. Just the left cheek. For my screensaver. See. (*Showing* CARL *the phone.*) The big red mouth with the tongue sticking out.

CARL (*refusing to look*). I know it alright.

BUSH. I was on that like a shot, Carl. I never knew Mick Jagger's lips would be that soft.

CARL. You're a dirtbird, Busher. A fucking dirtbird.

BUSH. Two-and-a-half hours later I pull back out of the driveway. I can't sit in the seat properly. I get two more poxy jobs and head back home. I was shattered. Fucking ridiculous. Thirty euro for the night's work. Hardly covers the diesel. Just not right, is it?

GEORGE. No it's not, Bush, but it's easily explained.

BUSH. Is it?

GEORGE. Yes – you're a pervert.

CARL. That's an addiction there, Bush.

BUSH. To what?

CARL. To…

BUSH. Women?

CARL. Danger.

BUSH. Stop.

CARL. Sex. You're a... (*Searching for the word*.)

GEORGE. Pervert.

CARL. Nymphomaniac.

BUSH. Would the two of yis go and fuck off.

CARL. And you are going to get yourself killed if you're not careful. 'Right Said Fred' Farrell might not be the sharpest knife in the toolbox, but the man's a genius when it comes to cracking heads.

BUSH. I know he is. But I can never seem to help meself. I just don't know. I'd stick my prick in a guillotine if it had blonde hair and big tits.

CARL. That's the definition of an addict right there.

BUSH. No, Carl – that's the definition of most normal, everyday, run-of-the-mill fellas I know – present company of you two sad bastards excluded.

Pause.

GEORGE. We're going to have to go over to his house now.

CARL. Are you mad? Fred will kill him.

GEORGE. Fuck Fred. That's his problem. I'm talking about Jackie. You said he wants paying tonight.

CARL. He was very strong about that.

GEORGE. Then tonight it has to be. That's more important than the money itself.

CARL. Do you have three grand to give me, George?

GEORGE. No I don't –

CARL. Then...

GEORGE. I have some. Maybe half of it. We'll have to swing by the house. (*To* BUSH.) What about you?

BUSH. Jaysus. Just what's in my pockets. Couple of hundred.

BUSH gives GEORGE the contents of his pockets.

CARL. Thanks, Bush.

GEORGE. Okay. Not too far off. What about your dad?

CARL. I phoned him already.

GEORGE. And?

CARL. He said it's time for him to be cruel to be kind with me.

GEORGE. So he knew and I didn't?

CARL. I'm sorry, George.

GEORGE. Right. We'll just have to go with what we have for now. Tell him we'll have the rest by the weekend. Then we go straight out and earn it.

CARL. I don't know, George.

GEORGE. What don't you know?

CARL. It never sounded like there was a lot of love lost between the two of you. We might be making things a lot worse here.

GEORGE. It doesn't sound like that's possible to me. Let's go.

CARL and GEORGE stand to leave.

BUSH (*rising to join them*). Stall the ball.

GEORGE. What are you doing?

BUSH. I'm going with yis.

CARL. You're what?

BUSH. I wouldn't miss this shit for the world.

CARL. I'm a dead man.

Blackout.

Scene Three

JACKIE*'s house.* JACKIE *and* FRED *are preparing to go out.*

FRED. It's dark enough.

JACKIE. Have you got your keys?

FRED. We're not taking my car.

JACKIE. Why not?

FRED. You don't think it might stand out?

JACKIE. You couldn't get a proper normal car, could you?

FRED. We'll go in yours.

JACKIE. My arse we will. I get stopped every night. Fucking routine with them.

FRED. Well, we're not going there on pushbikes.

JACKIE. Don't be smart. It doesn't suit you.

FRED. Rob one?

JACKIE. That's just pure Mensa stuff, that is. As if it's not bad enough we'll go down there in a stolen car.

FRED. I'm just thinking out loud.

JACKIE. Well, don't. If you've nothing helpful to say, nothing intelligent to contribute – because, seriously, don't just speak to hear the sound of your own voice. It's not that easy on the ears.

FRED. So what then?

JACKIE. I'll call a cab.

FRED. A taxi?

JACKIE. Best cover we could have. Lay low in the back. Anyone asks – we're out looking for a party to go to.

FRED. Yeah – good thinking.

JACKIE. Thanks.

JACKIE leaves. FRED checks a handwritten map he has prepared. There is a soft, tentative knock. FRED answers. GEORGE is in the doorway.

FRED. Uncle George.

GEORGE. Freddie.

FRED. Jesus.

GEORGE. Yeah.

FRED. Come in. Come in.

GEORGE enters, followed by CARL and BUSH.

Pause.

It's good to see you.

GEORGE. You too, son.

FRED is slightly emotional.

Come here to me.

GEORGE and FRED hug awkwardly. CARL and BUSH exchange amazed looks.

FRED. How have you been keeping with yourself?

GEORGE. I've had a bit of a rough time with it all, Freddie.

FRED. So me dad keeps saying.

GEORGE. Look at the size of you standing there.

FRED. Ahh.

GEORGE. What did you go and do to yourself?

FRED. Just pumping away at the aul' iron. Bulking myself up.

GEORGE. Big time.

FRED. Turning all that old fat of mine into muscle. Like my aul' fella always says – you can't do nothing 'bout the brains God gave you, but you can control your body at least. We can all do that.

GEORGE. I suppose we can.

FRED. You know the way he bangs on at me.

GEORGE. I remember.

FRED. Yeah...

GEORGE. And all your lovely hair.

FRED. It's just the fashion these days.

GEORGE. I wouldn't know you, Freddie.

FRED. I haven't changed that much, for fuck's sake.

GEORGE. No – I'd have passed you on the street if I saw you, and if I ever have I'm sorry because I swear to God that wasn't intentional. You understand.

FRED. Don't worry about it.

Pause.

GEORGE. Your dad home?

FRED. He is, yeah.

GEORGE. I came over for Carl.

FRED. I see.

CARL. Alright, Fred.

FRED. Carl.

GEORGE. So...

FRED (*to* CARL). Are you sure this is a good idea?

CARL. It's not my idea.

GEORGE. Will you give him a shout for us, son?

FRED. Of course. (*To* BUSH.) What are you doing here with this?

BUSH. I'm not too sure myself, Fred.

FRED. Are you alright again for this weekend – with the runs?

BUSH. I can't wait.

FRED. A dirty little bastard, this one.

GEORGE. We know, we know.

BUSH. Tell your wife I was asking for her.

FRED. What's that?

GEORGE. Bush.

BUSH. Your Jasmine. Make sure and tell her I said hi.

FRED (*to* GEORGE). As if she'd even know who he was.

GEORGE. Gobshite.

> FRED *exits*.

CARL. For fuck's sake, Bush.

BUSH. What?

CARL. You'll get us all killed.

BUSH. I'm only having a laugh.

GEORGE (*to both*). Keep it down, the both of you.

CARL. I haven't the bottle for this, George.

GEORGE. We've come this far now.

BUSH. Relax, for fuck's sake.

CARL. No – it's gone on me altogether.

GEORGE. Just hold your nerve here, Carl.

CARL. I think I'm going to be sick.

BUSH. Talk about a drama queen.

> JACKIE *enters, followed by* FRED.

JACKIE. Well, the dead arose and appeared to many. It's all happening around here today. Look at you. Looking well, Georgie-Boy.

GEORGE. Jackie.

JACKIE. Straight and narrow with never a slip. So I hear.

GEORGE. Fifteen years now.

JACKIE. It's not – is it?

GEORGE. Coming up on, yeah.

JACKIE. Since…

GEORGE. Evelyn.

JACKIE. Lord rest her.

Pause.

And your Jenny too, of course.

GEORGE. Of course.

JACKIE. My God.

GEORGE. Yeah.

JACKIE. I was very sorry to hear about her. That's the truth now.

GEORGE. I know it is.

JACKIE. I sent a wreath.

GEORGE. So…

JACKIE. So – clean as a whistle.

GEORGE. Trying my best.

JACKIE. Good for you.

GEORGE. Cheers.

JACKIE. And all your debts paid off? Apart from mine, that is.

GEORGE. I'm nearly there.

JACKIE. Story of your life, isn't it, George?

GEORGE. Yours too maybe.

JACKIE. Maybe. I never thought of it like that. And I honestly never thought you'd set foot in this house either. I'd have lost a bet with you there.

GEORGE. Nice place.

JACKIE. Glad you like it.

GEORGE. Bungalow, yeah?

JACKIE. Best for Carmel.

GEORGE. She well?

JACKIE. She's worse.

GEORGE. Pity…

JACKIE. That's how it works.

GEORGE. Still…

Pause.

JACKIE. Cost me three million last year.

GEORGE. It looks it. Really does.

JACKIE. I wouldn't get two for it now.

GEORGE. No.

JACKIE. But all of life's a gamble, isn't it, Georgie?

GEORGE. You've certainly come a long way, Jack.

JACKIE. I'd a fucking long way to come.

GEORGE. Only in your own head.

JACKIE. Well, that's all that counts in the end, isn't it?

GEORGE. Other things count too.

JACKIE. To you they do, George. They always did. But take a good look around at where we both finished up and tell me – were your other things worth it? Are they really any good to you now it's nearly all over? Because I always wanted you with me. You had that chance from the get-go. Tell me the God's honest, now that you're here in front of me – no regrets at all?

GEORGE. I didn't spend six years of my life in prison.

Pause.

JACKIE. And who the fuck is this then, Carl?

CARL. Just a cousin of mine.

JACKIE. Just a cousin, yeah?

CARL. 'Two in the Bush.'

JACKIE. Beg your pardon?

FRED. Always has a bird in his hand. Isn't that right?

BUSH. That's where I got it from, Fred. Just 'Bush' for short, though. To all my friends. Nice to meet you, Mr Farrell.

   BUSH *extends his hand.* JACKIE *blanks him.*

JACKIE. So tell me now, Carl, because it's just starting to dawn on me, what am I faced with here?

CARL. I'm not with you, Jackie.

JACKIE. A show of force?

BUSH. Not at all – we just want to…

JACKIE. You speak when you're fucking spoken to.

BUSH. I certainly will.

JACKIE. Is this supposed to intimidate me? You and your henchmen?

CARL. No, Jackie. That's not what this is at all. They're here to…

JACKIE. What?

CARL. Just to…

JACKIE. Protect you, is it? Is that it? Do you need protection, Carl?

CARL. I don't know if I do or I don't, I just want to talk to you.

JACKIE. I thought we did all our talking today.

CARL. We did, of course, but…

JACKIE. Well, Freddie, it looks like we're outnumbered – Are you scared?

FRED. No.

JACKIE. Because I have to say I'm fucking pissing my pants right now.

GEORGE. Calm down.

JACKIE. Don't tell me what to do, George. Remember the last time you came round to a place of mine shouting the odds.

GEORGE. I remember.

JACKIE. Good. Keep that front and centre. (*Points at his forehead.*) Right here. And maybe we won't have any trouble.

BUSH. There won't be any trouble –

JACKIE. I'll be the fucking judge of that –

GEORGE. We just need to talk to you. A few minutes of your time. That's all.

JACKIE. Well, I wish I had a few minutes, George. Really I do – we could sit, drink a glass of whiskey and chat about all the times we had back in the day. Believe it or not, I'd enjoy that a great deal. But I'm pushed for time right now, so I'm afraid I'll have to move along to the business in hand. Where's my fucking money, Carl?

GEORGE. We need to come to some sort of arrangement about it.

JACKIE (*to* CARL). Don't you do this to me.

GEORGE. I have a proposal for you. I think you'll be happy with it.

JACKIE (*to* CARL). Don't you dare tell me you haven't got it with you. Not after today. I won't be able to handle it. I'm liable to crack up.

GEORGE. I've got most of it with me. Right here. And the rest we'll…

JACKIE. Jesus fucking Christ. Am I speaking English? Seriously – Fred, you were here, was I clear this morning or was there some confusion?

FRED. You were very clear. He was very clear, George.

JACKIE. And you're a clever man, Carl. An educated man. So it's just plain obvious to me now – you refuse to take me

seriously when I've stopped laughing. And I have to tell you
– and I know George will back me up on this despite himself
– that's a mistake on your part.

CARL. I'm taking you seriously, Jackie.

BUSH. Seriously, he is.

JACKIE. See, you say that and you say a lot of other things, but
actions speak volumes and this is the effort you made today.
After all your bullshit. You went straight to him, had a little
moan and he told you what he always tells anyone who'll
listen to him – fuck me because I'm full of shit.

GEORGE. I didn't tell him that.

JACKIE. No, but you told him you'd come over here and sort
me out.

GEORGE. I told him I'd come over here and ask you for some
more time.

JACKIE. Asked and answered. By him. This morning.

GEORGE. I told him that you might change your mind about
that for...

JACKIE. For...

GEORGE. For me. For...

JACKIE. What?

GEORGE. Old time's sake.

JACKIE. Ahh, there it is. I could fucking see it coming a mile
off.

GEORGE. Remember who you're talking to now.

JACKIE. What have I always told you about that, George?

GEORGE. I know what you told me and I haven't come here
empty-handed. I've brought you every last penny I have and
I don't even have this. I am standing here, cap in hand. Is
that not enough?

JACKIE. What's enough? – It's still short, isn't it?

GEORGE. It's short of what he owes at this moment in time, yes, but...

JACKIE. But you shouldn't have bothered your bollocks bringing it. It's just the same old same old – and you above all others should know, George – this isn't about his or your fucking money. I don't need your little peace offering. Look around you, for fuck's sake, I don't even need his poxy three grand. It's not a question of that and it never was. What I need is for people like you and him to stop taking me for granted.

GEORGE. This isn't about you and me now...

JACKIE. To start making an effort with me because I don't deserve any less.

GEORGE. And no one is saying you fucking do, alright.

JACKIE. This is just contempt –

for me –

from you –

all over again.

Same shit as fifteen fucking years ago.

GEORGE. Jackie.

JACKIE. Just basic bad manners. And that was always the one thing that you could never stand, George. So how do you expect me to? How are you that arrogant with me?

GEORGE. Don't start reading it like that because that's not what this is at all.

JACKIE. This is downright rudeness of the highest order and it's my own fault because I'm too tolerant.

GEORGE. Give it over.

JACKIE. Well, I'm making a resolution right here, right now. From this moment forward I am going to be more assertive. Fred, you're on.

He throws FRED *his bat.*

It's time to hammer the point home to the boys here.

BUSH. Oh Jaysus – hold the phone, lads.

CARL. This wasn't a good idea, George.

JACKIE. It was the worst you ever had.

GEORGE. Put the bat down, Fred.

FRED *moves instinctively to put the bat down.*

JACKIE. Fred.

FRED *picks up the bat again.* JACKIE *turns to* GEORGE.

Now don't you dare give another order in this house. Do you hear me?

GEORGE. Put it down, son.

FRED (*confused*). Dad.

JACKIE. George, I am fucking warning you.

GEORGE. Don't do this. Hear me out, Jackie. I'm minding my manners here. I'm not roaring and shouting. I'm not calling any names. I'm not throwing any digs. I am here to ask you for a favour. I know you don't have to do it, but I'm saying please. Please listen. And you can take this whatever way you have to take it, but I'm saying it anyway – you owe me and you know it.

JACKIE. I owe you?

GEORGE. Bring Carmel in here now. We'll ask her whether you do or not.

Pause. JACKIE *nods to* FRED *to put down the bat.*

JACKIE. Alright, you want to talk – we'll talk.

GEORGE. Thank you.

JACKIE. But let's establish the field we're playing on first –

GEORGE. Fine.

JACKIE. And I'm speaking to you collectively now, because you all decided to show up here and take responsibility, right?

GEORGE. Right.

JACKIE (*to* BUSH). Right?

BUSH. Absolutely.

JACKIE. So it's simple then – you lot owe me three grand which is due tonight. And I owe you fuck-all. Especially you, George. Whatever you did for this family was greatly appreciated by all. But you took it back in spades with interest when you decided to give me the two fingers and renege on your bill in the full public glare. So we are more than quits as far as that goes. Clear?

GEORGE. Clear.

JACKIE. Good – Alright – Well, we've all just had a stressful few minutes, so let's sit down and take a breath because you never know – there actually might be a way we can get through this – right, Fred?

FRED. Right.

JACKIE. You want some tea?

GEORGE. No, thank you – we're alright.

BUSH. I'm parched actually.

GEORGE. Shut up.

JACKIE. Carl – you want something to eat? You hungry? You're probably hungry, right?

CARL. No, I'm fine, Jackie.

JACKIE. You look hungry.

BUSH. The last thing he looks is hungry.

JACKIE. You want a sandwich?

CARL. No, really.

JACKIE. It's no trouble. There's ham, chicken, roast beef – Fridge is full, so go and take your pick.

CARL. I won't. Trying to cut back. Maybe we could just...

JACKIE. Get down to business.

CARL. If you don't mind.

JACKIE. I like your style.

> GEORGE *hands over an envelope*.

GEORGE. There's eighteen hundred there. So that's twelve hundred left. And the plan is we'll...

JACKIE (*throwing the envelope back*). Keep it.

GEORGE. Keep it?

JACKIE. I'm not interested.

GEORGE. You're not.

JACKIE. All or nothing, like I said.

GEORGE. Well, we don't have it all, so – where do we go from here?

JACKIE. We move on to my plan.

GEORGE. You have a plan?

JACKIE. That's the only reason we're still talking and not tearing strips off each other, Georgie.

GEORGE. I should have guessed.

JACKIE. So – it's what we in the world of business refer to as a win-win situation. For us all.

BUSH. Sounds very promising, Mr Farrell.

JACKIE. You need to talk an awful lot less.

BUSH. I think that's a fair comment.

GEORGE. What is it? Your plan.

JACKIE. You work it off.

GEORGE. Well, that's sort of what I'm talking about, isn't it? But it'll take a bit of time. Just a day or two.

JACKIE. You work it off tonight. Right now.

GEORGE. And how do we do that?

JACKIE. You do a little run for me. And I pay you three grand to do it. Works everything out nice and rosy, doesn't it?

BUSH. It certainly seems to.

CARL. Hold on a minute now.

GEORGE. Where's the run to?

JACKIE. Tullamore.

GEORGE. And who am I driving?

JACKIE. You're not driving anyone.

GEORGE. Jackie.

JACKIE. You're bringing Carl along with you for the spin. Lover boy is staying with me and Fred until you two get back safe and sound. Call him our insurance policy.

BUSH. Sounds like a solid plan to me, boys.

GEORGE. If we're not carrying anyone else with us – what are we doing?

JACKIE. You're doing a pick-up.

GEORGE. Of?

JACKIE. A bag.

GEORGE. What kind of a fucking bag?

JACKIE. Fred.

FRED. It's black. Leather. Basic. Like a holdall, you know. It's wedged in up under the base of a hedge. On a back road behind the town. It's all here for you –

He hands him the piece of paper with the map.

JACKIE. So I just need you to go down there now, get it and bring it back here. When you do – the debt's forgiven, this arsehole goes free and everyone is happy as pigshite.

BUSH. Fantastic.

CARL. You're having us on, right?

JACKIE (*to* GEORGE). You know I'm not.

CARL. This just gets worse and worse.

FRED. What's your problem, Carl?

CARL. We can't get involved in this kind of shite, Jackie.

JACKIE. What kind of shite would that be?

CARL. Look, I'm not stupid.

JACKIE. Oh, I know you're not, Carl. We're all sick of hearing how fucking clever you are, aren't we?

FRED. Yes, we are.

JACKIE. Question is, are you clever enough to play the best hand to come your way in a long time? What's it to be?

CARL. No.

JACKIE. No?

CARL. Fuck it. No. I'll just take the hiding.

FRED. That's that sorted then. We'll see you tomorrow, Carl. Pop over here round noon. We need to get a move on, Dad.

BUSH. No one's taking any hiding. What's the big deal, lads? I sit here in a cosy chair. You two go and pick up a poxy bag. All over in a few hours. Piece of cake. Get yourselves going will you.

CARL. I'll go myself, so. No need for the lads to get dragged into it. I'll go now. Give me that map, George.

JACKIE. Not an option, Carl. It's a two-man job. Second man sits in the back as a fare. That's the cover. And I'm keeping him here while you're gone. Management technique. Motivation for the two of you to run it smoothly.

CARL. It's way too risky, lads.

JACKIE. There's no risk in this, George. Look at me. No risk at all because you know nothing about any of it. You're completely innocent. Just doing a run. What you do every day for a living. As long as you go straight there, pick it up, leave it closed – And I cannot stress this enough, George – you do not open that fucking bag. Under any circumstances. As long as you do all that, you're untouchable.

CARL. There must be some other way to sort this out, Jack.

JACKIE. This is it. The only game in town and I will consider it the height of ignorance if you turn me down. I'll take offence from all of you not just him. And you know what happens then.

GEORGE. Thirty grand.

JACKIE. Excuse me?

GEORGE. On top of the debt wiped. He has credit cards, loans, all sorts to pay. Thirty grand for the run.

JACKIE. This is not a negotiation, George.

GEORGE. It's worth it to you, isn't it? To get this done right, and that's how we'll do it. I know what happened in Tullamore today, Jackie. It's all over the news. I know how much you're after getting away with. So whatever's in that bag – it's worth thirty grand to you, minimum.

The doorbell rings. FRED *answers it.*

FRED. It's the taxi you called.

JACKIE. Ten grand. As a gesture. Yes-or-no territory now. What's it to be?

GEORGE (*re: the taxi driver*). Give him a fiver, Freddie. Tell him you're sorry. We won't be needing him.

Blackout.

End of Act One.

ACT TWO

Scene One

CARL *and* GEORGE *in a field behind Tullamore, staring at the bag on the ground.*

CARL. You think that's it.

GEORGE. That's it.

CARL. It's not in the hedge, though.

GEORGE. That's it.

CARL. So.

GEORGE. So?

CARL. So let's get the fuck out of here then, yeah?

CARL *moves to pick up the bag.*

GEORGE. Hold your horses.

CARL. For what?

GEORGE. We are going to take our time with this, Carl.

CARL. Surely that's precisely what we're not going to do, George.

GEORGE. We're going to take our time and establish exactly where we are here.

CARL. Are you feeling alright?

GEORGE. And exactly what we're doing.

CARL. We need to get a move on.

GEORGE. So, you tell me – what are we doing? Here? Now? You and me?

CARL. What's this about?

GEORGE. What are we doing?

CARL. George?

GEORGE. What are we doing?

CARL. Our jobs. Alright.

GEORGE. Carl.

CARL. What? What do you want me to say?

GEORGE. The truth. That's all. No more. No less.

CARL. We're on a run. A paid run. Pick up a bag. This fucking
bag. Now can we please just pick it up and get ourselves
motoring to fuck?

GEORGE. Don't touch it.

CARL. Excuse me?

GEORGE. Not yet.

CARL. This isn't happening to me. We need to leave.

GEORGE. We're not rushing this. Or I will blow it all wide
open, I swear to God. Now we are going to stand here and
have a little heart to heart. Breathe in this fresh country air.
It'll do us both the world of good.

CARL. I don't get it, George. I really don't.

GEORGE. Then try harder, Carl – You're going to attempt to
tell me that we are just doing our work here?

CARL. Exactly, yes.

GEORGE (*indicating the bag*). That that there's just another
fare?

CARL. That's the best way to look at it, isn't it?

GEORGE. That we are doing nothing wrong in the wide world.

CARL. That's the only way I can cope with it all, George, so...

GEORGE. We're accessories, Carl.

CARL. Ahh, don't now...

GEORGE. After the fact.

CARL. Please.

GEORGE. To a very serious crime.

CARL. George.

GEORGE. An armed robbery to be precise. This here is everything I have spent my life avoiding.

CARL. There's no need for this.

GEORGE. There's every need. Now you can stand there and pretend you know fuck-all to your heart's content – fine – but you know. You've heard the news on the radio on the way down here, the same as me. Quarter of a million is robbed…

CARL. Ah, for Christ's sake.

GEORGE. Quarter of a million is robbed from a Securicor van in Tullamore this morning. And now we're on a run for Jackie Farrell to pick up a bag that was dumped on the outskirts. We're not to open it. We're not to ask any questions. Right so far? Now, you're the maths teacher, Carl – I'm open to correction – but that two and two is giving me four.

CARL. We don't know for certain that this has anything to do with any of that.

GEORGE. Well, what are the odds? Mr Gambling Man? Because I'll bet they're pretty low. Right?

CARL. Why are you doing this to me?

GEORGE. Because I want you to take a good look around – and tell me where you are, Carl.

CARL. Where I am?

GEORGE. Where are you, son?

CARL. Jesus Christ.

GEORGE. Where are you?

CARL. I'm in the back arse of the middle of fucking nowhere, George. Same place as you.

GEORGE. You're at the bottom. And I'm your welcome committee. I'll try my best to make your stay here as brief as possible.

CARL. We're going to get ourselves caught.

GEORGE. I want you to take a good look around at the lowest point in your life, Carl.

CARL. There's nothing surer.

GEORGE. You probably thought it was the day Jenny passed.

CARL. Of course it was, for fuck's sake.

GEORGE. No. Seems that was just when your fall started in earnest. You kept on dropping. But it stops now. Because it has to. This here is rock bottom. Nowhere further down you can go except underground in a coffin, and that's not an option, so this is a good day.

CARL. This is anything but a good day.

GEORGE. When you look back it will be.

But we need to do this right and it won't take long.

The most important thing is that you recognise it for what it is.

It's different for us all. Some are lucky. Some hit it standing in the hallway, reading the first warning notice from the bank. Start climbing back up before things get really out of hand. Me and you – we're special types. We're the kind they write the songs about – we fall as low as you can go.

CARL. Me and you?

GEORGE. Carl – all of this here is history repeating itself at a frightening rate. I inflicted the very worst this dirty plague has to offer on my family for more than five years. And I lost the job lot, up to and including the very roof over our heads.

CARL. Jesus, George.

GEORGE. But I'm still here despite it all. I'm realising now that I'm going to have to start appreciating that fact. And I'm determined that you are too.

That's why I need you to remember this place. Here. Remember how it looks, sounds, smells, but most of all remember how you feel in the pit of your stomach right this minute – after you've gone and lost everything you have worked so hard all your life to put together.

After you've been reduced to this place because this night you're no better than a toerag. Remember this feeling for ever.

Because it's the only thing that can cure you. You call it up whenever you feel a weakness and it'll make you strong as an ox, I promise you.

You'll be back here many times in your head over the course of the rest of your days. Back in the middle of nowhere behind Tullamore town, feeling sick as sick can be.

This is it. Where it all ends and where it starts again. Okay?

CARL. I'll fix it. I'll do whatever it takes.

GEORGE. What it takes is you and me sitting in Gardiner Street tomorrow lunchtime at a GA meeting. Your first of many.

CARL. Right.

GEORGE. Right – time for step one.

CARL. My name is Carl and I'm…

GEORGE. Fuck all that for the moment. Our step one now – get you clear. Back in the black as soon as we can. Starting with this bag back safe and sound.

CARL. Maybe we should leave it behind us, George.

GEORGE. We should what?

CARL. You're right about it all and I'm so sorry I've brought us to this. But we've done nothing wrong yet. Let's say we couldn't find it. Walk away now. What's the worst that could happen?

GEORGE. I've no desire to find out, Carl.

GEORGE *reaches to pick up the bag.*

CARL. Wait a second, though.

GEORGE. I thought we were in a hurry, Carl.

CARL. What do you think is in it?

GEORGE. I'm trying my damnedest not to think about that, to tell you the truth.

GEORGE goes to pick it up again.

CARL. Do you think it's the guns?

GEORGE. What fucking guns?

CARL. That they used today. They probably dumped them when they were finished and now they're starting to panic because they can be traced back somehow.

GEORGE. Well, I never thought of that, but...

CARL. Odds are...

GEORGE. Pretty low alright.

CARL. Could just be the clothes they wore, though, couldn't it?

GEORGE. It could. Yeah.

GEORGE goes to pick up the bag again.

CARL. Or explosives.

GEORGE. For fuck's sake, Carl.

CARL. Well, they used some sort of Semtex to blow the doors off, didn't they?

GEORGE. Yes – they did.

Pause. They crouch to look at the bag. CARL's phone beeps with a text message and they jump.

Jesus.

CARL (*looking at the text*). Bush.

GEORGE. What is it?

CARL. You don't want to know.

GEORGE. Is he alright?

CARL. I actually think he's enjoying this.

GEORGE. Man's a fucking lunatic.

CARL. There has to be some other way, George.

GEORGE. Well, I don't have one for you, so...

CARL. If we just think it through.

GEORGE. The time for thinking's long gone as far as this shit goes, son.

CARL. What did he owe you?

GEORGE. Who? – Jackie?

CARL. Must have been something substantial because I thought all hell was about to break loose back there.

GEORGE. None of that is going to help us down here, Carl.

CARL. It might, though – what was it all about?

GEORGE. Long time ago now. Back in the day when he got banged up for the fraud.

CARL. Fraud?

GEORGE. Insurance scam. Staging car crashes all over the city. Fellas claiming for whiplash and bad backs. He wanted me to go in on it with him. But I wouldn't. I think he blamed me when he got caught. I wasn't there for him.

CARL. They gave him six years in prison for fraud?

GEORGE. No – he got two for that. First week in he gets in a row and beats some poor fucker to death with a broom handle. He got another four consecutive for manslaughter, and he served every day of both sentences. 'Good behaviour' never applied to Jackie Farrell.

CARL. No.

GEORGE. And for those six years I called to his house every Monday and gave Carmel money for the week. I cut his grass, washed his windows, put out his bins. I picked up little

Freddie from school if it was raining and cleared his
driveway if it snowed. I helped keep the show on the road
for him. We were friends, you see. Best friends.

CARL. What happened?

GEORGE. In a nutshell – he got released and started opening
up casinos and I became an out-and-out gambling addict and
started losing like a mad man in them.

CARL. Not a great combination.

GEORGE. To say the least.

CARL. But if you two were such good friends, couldn't you...

GEORGE. That only goes so far. Especially with Jackie. And he
was completely different with me from his first day out.
Didn't want me anywhere near Carmel or Freddie. Especially
Freddie. And I took offence to that. I really did because I
didn't deserve it. I didn't deserve any of the shit going on in
my life back then. Especially not my poor wife wasting away
in front of my eyes. Addict never deserves what's happening
to him, you see. Nothing's ever fair to a gambler.

CARL. How bad did it get on you?

GEORGE. It was appalling. I owed everyone. And I was selling
everything I had to pay them. Except for him. Him, I kept
telling to write it off and stop annoying me. Terrible carry-on.

Then the day Evelyn died, I left the hospital with Jenny in
tow, no more than twelve or thirteen she was, and I drove
straight to his old club in Rathmines.

Sat myself down at the blackjack table –

Sat Jenny on the chair beside me –

And lost ten grand in one hour flat.

I refused to stick, no matter what was dealt.

Jack and an eight – 'Hit me' –

Queen and a nine –'Hit me' –

Pair of fucking Kings – 'Hit me' –

Jenny sobbing away to herself.

When my credit was well and truly bust, they called Jackie down.

He asked me outside for a quiet word. Pinned me up against a wall in the alley. Told me to get a fucking grip and go home. Said he'd ignore what had just happened inside in light of the day that was in it – but all my other debts to him stood and he wanted them paid pronto. I started screaming at him. Told him he could fucking sing for it all because he could never put a price on everything I'd done for him. Then I slapped him. Hard. Across the cheek. Jenny let out a little cry. She was always fond of her Uncle Jackie.

He went back inside. Came out with his blue bat. And in the space of two minutes I had broken both my wrists and all my fingers from punching his face and head. Left him deaf in his right ear. And he had managed to break my arms, six of my ribs, puncture my lung and I still have trouble pissing to this day.

CARL. Fuck.

GEORGE. And the two of us ended up stretched out on the muck and dirt in the rain and sleet. I was looking across the puddles at him looking back at me, listening to my little girl screaming her lungs out.

That was when I hit the bottom. At long last.

And it was Jackie that was with me. My little Jenny too, God be good to her.

CARL. She never said a word to me about any of it, George.

Pause.

GEORGE. It's time now, Carl.

CARL (*indicating the bag*). We should open it first at least.

GEORGE. We're not opening it. This here is phase one in getting you right. We do this by the book, like we were told. Then we'll move onwards and upwards if our luck is back in.

CARL. But we need to know what we're dealing with.

GEORGE. I already know exactly what we're dealing with, thanks very much.

CARL. I mean the basics, like where do we carry it in the car? How to handle a situation if it occurs. I have to think of you in all this.

GEORGE. I'm telling you now – we open that bag and he'll know.

CARL. We can always close it back up, George. That's the miracle of zips.

GEORGE. He'll know. No matter what you do or say. He will look you in your eye and he'll fucking know.

CARL. I'm opening it.

GEORGE. We're at the end of the cycle now, Carl. Remember. Rock bottom. We open that bag and it could all start back up again.

GEORGE *and* CARL *stare at the bag.*

Blackout.

Scene Two

JACKIE's *house.* BUSH *and* FRED *are there.* JACKIE *is off-stage in the kitchen.*

BUSH. So what's in the bag?

FRED. Mind your business, Bush.

BUSH. Come on, we're not children, you can tell me – what's in it?

FRED. It's best you don't know – for your own sake.

BUSH. Must be important, though. Is it important?

FRED. Yes it's important. It's very fucking important.

BUSH. I knew it.

FRED. Just leave it at that.

Pause.

BUSH. Turn on the telly.

FRED. There's nothing on.

BUSH. No sport?

FRED. I hate sport.

BUSH. What, all sport?

FRED. Yes, all sport.

BUSH. How can anyone hate sport?

FRED. I don't see the fucking point in it.

BUSH. Fair enough.

Pause.

So what do you like?

FRED. On the telly?

BUSH. Yeah.

FRED. I like the documentaries.

BUSH. Me too.

FRED. Good for educating yourself.

BUSH. Absolutely. I watch a lot of the History Channel.

FRED. I like *Big Brother.*

BUSH. I see.

FRED. I watch that every year.

BUSH. I never got into it myself.

FRED. *I'm a Celebrity… Get Me Out of Here!*

BUSH. I must have missed that one too.

FRED. And you said you liked documentaries.

BUSH. Yes, but, well, they're not really, you know – documentaries – are they? – Not in the real sense of the...

FRED. You know the best one I've ever seen?

BUSH. What?

FRED. *The Swan.*

BUSH. Never heard of it.

FRED. Great programme.

BUSH. Really?

FRED. They take these women, you see, these pig-ugly fat fucking women – I mean, you need to see these birds to understand. You wouldn't go near them if your life depended on it.

And you know what they do? – They lock them away for three months solid. Put them on a serious diet. Stick them on a treadmill – eight hours a day, seven days a week.

And best of all – the real key to all of it – they give each of them as much plastic surgery as is deemed necessary.

Nothing is ruled out.

And at the end of the programme, these women, they're brought back on – and you wouldn't fucking believe it. The way they look. It's a miracle of modern science. Nothing less.

They've lost the weight, toned themselves up.

Their noses are straight, double chins gone.

They've got brand new sets of tits and lips.

Their hair is dyed blonde and they've been hosed down with a bucketload of fake tan – and it is a fucking miracle the way these dogs end up. You would get a boner looking at them with their clothes on.

Now that is good television.

BUSH. Sounds fucking magic.

FRED. Because it proves there's no need for it. In this day and age there is just no need for a woman to be walking around looking like a bag of spanners. There are things that can be done. Procedures that can be carried out. Three months is nothing – is it?

BUSH. No, it's not.

FRED. I ran into an ex-girlfriend of mine last Christmas, doing the shopping down Henry Street.

BUSH. I love it when that happens.

FRED. She must have put on four fucking stone since we were together.

BUSH. I hate that.

FRED. I nearly got physically sick.

BUSH. I can imagine.

FRED. Because people forget, you see. The way she looked when I was with her. They just see how she appears in the cold light of today and it reflects piss poorly on the principles of how I live my life. I didn't sleep a wink that night.

BUSH. I don't blame you.

FRED. And there's no excuse for us either, mind. None at all. What men like Carl are doing to themselves is just not fucking good enough.

BUSH. I couldn't agree more.

FRED. Standards must be maintained and that's all there is to it. That's why I keep myself in the shape I'm in.

BUSH. Great shape I have to say, and I don't mean anything by saying it.

FRED. You think looking like this comes easy?

BUSH. I wouldn't imagine so.

FRED. Make no mistake. This has taken work. Six days a week in the gym – hard graft – no fucking joke. Regular sunbed sessions. All-over wax once a month. I bleach my teeth every week and I shave my head every day. It's about respecting yourself, you see. Respect for your body.

BUSH. Absolutely.

FRED. You know, my missus has had two boob jobs and a tummy tuck already. She's thirty-four and she looks twenty-one.

BUSH. She's a peach.

FRED. You want to get yourself a woman like that, Bush?

BUSH. Every fucking night.

FRED. Well, now you know what you have to do.

BUSH. Thanks for the tip, Fred.

FRED. You're welcome.

JACKIE *enters.*

JACKIE. Your friends better get here soon.

BUSH. They're only gone.

JACKIE. They're gone since five o'clock. It's after eight. Tullamore's down the fucking road.

BUSH. I'll send them a text.

JACKIE. Put your phone away. What did I say, Fred? No communication whatsoever.

BUSH. Fair enough.

JACKIE. Don't tell me you've been texting them.

BUSH. No.

JACKIE. Have you?

BUSH. No.

JACKIE. Has he?

FRED. I don't think he has.

JACKIE. Give me the phone.

FRED *takes* BUSH's *phone and hands it to* JACKIE.

BUSH. Okay, I might have.

JACKIE. Unbelievable.

BUSH. Just an aul' joke. Nothing related.

JACKIE (*reading out the text*). 'Jaysus, lads, Mick Jagger's lips just won't stop calling me.'

BUSH. You'd have had to have been there.

JACKIE. It must be just me.

> JACKIE *hands the phone back to* FRED. FRED *is handing the phone back to* BUSH *when he notices the screensaver.*

FRED. You a Rolling Stones fan, yeah?

BUSH (*oblivious*). No, I can't stand them.

FRED. You've got their logo on your phone.

BUSH (*realises and is petrified*). I know.

FRED. My wife loves them.

BUSH. Is that right?

FRED. She's actually got that tattooed on her arse.

JACKIE. For fuck's sake, Fred – I don't need to be hearing about your wife's arse. (*Taking out his Lotto ticket.*) Put on the Lotto.

FRED. It's well over by now. (*Re: the phone.*) It's funny, you know...

BUSH. Throw me the phone, Fred.

FRED. What?

BUSH. Quick – I can check the Lotto on it – I get a text sent to me with the numbers straight after the draw. Quick. Quick.

JACKIE. Give him the phone.

> FRED *throws the phone back to* BUSH. *He starts to look for the numbers.*

BUSH. Here they are. Four, seven, nineteen, twenty-seven, twenty-eight, thirty-one.

JACKIE (*after checking*). Not one fucking number.

BUSH. Bonus is twelve. Do you want the Plus?

JACKIE. Fuck the Plus.

FRED. Let me see that phone again, Bush.

BUSH (*holding on to the phone*). I could have told you not to bother with the Lotto tonight. It's never won at the two million mark.

JACKIE. Of course it is.

BUSH. They rig it, you see.

JACKIE. They don't fucking rig it.

FRED (*wants the phone*). Bush.

BUSH. I'm telling you, Jackie – the Lotto's rigged.

JACKIE. And I'm telling you – it can't be done. Alright. It's a random draw.

BUSH. Oh, it's random alright. I'm not arguing that. That's not the fix. They don't rig who wins it. They rig when it's won.

FRED. The phone.

JACKIE. And why in the name of Jaysus would they do that?

BUSH. Rollover.

JACKIE. Rollover.

BUSH. So it builds and builds.

JACKIE. Don't talk shite.

FRED. Just pass it to me for a second, will you.

BUSH. Freddie, how many people do you think'll do the Lotto this Saturday? Now that it's rolled over. How many?

FRED. Don't know.

BUSH. At least twice as many as played today, that's how many.

And it won't be won Saturday either and twice as many will play it next Wednesday. By Saturday week there'll be queues in every newsagents.

Now you think about it. How many people do you seriously think would play the Lotto if the jackpot was won every time and it was always two million flat?

FRED. You've got a point there.

JACKIE. Don't encourage him, Fred, for fuck's sake.

BUSH. And it actually costs them less. This is the genius of it. If it's won every time they get hit for two million a pop. If it rolls over they only have to add a million – and they get themselves more people playing into the bargain. The perfect scam.

JACKIE. Alright now. Time to knock it on the head with the Stockholm Syndrome. I'm tired of it – Fucking ridiculous.

BUSH. It's ridiculous to think that they wouldn't do it.

JACKIE. Enough.

BUSH. It would just be bad business on their behalf. And they are not bad businessmen. They're the state's bookie.

FRED. He's fucking spot on, Dad. And they call us gangsters.

JACKIE. But there's just one little problem with all of this bull-shit, isn't there? – How do they do it? How do they pull off this massive fraud on the entire nation week after week?

BUSH. The fifteen-minute delay.

JACKIE. What fucking fifteen-minute delay?

BUSH. The latest possible time that you can purchase a Lotto ticket is what?

FRED. Quarter to eight. No later. I've been caught out a few times.

BUSH. Quarter to eight. On the button. And the machine opera-tors have no choice. The machines shut down. They're pro-grammed to. At a quarter to eight. They programme them to shut down for the night.

JACKIE. So?

BUSH. So – why do they do that, Jackie? If it truly is a random draw? Why close down at a quarter to eight? Or ten to? Or five to? Why can't I buy a ticket right up until Ronan Collins pulls the first number?

FRED. I don't think he does it any more.

BUSH. Whoever then – Look – go to Shelbourne tonight, you can place a bet the second before the bunny passes the trap. Once your bet is recorded before the race begins, there's no difference.

So once my numbers are recorded in the Lotto at a minute to eight, what's the difference there? Why do they close it down fifteen minutes to go? Why do they need those fifteen minutes?

FRED. Why? Why? Why, Bush?

BUSH. Simple. It may not be enough time to rig a winner, but fifteen minutes is plenty of time to rig a loser.

The machine uses the time to identify every combination that has actually been played for that draw.

And then it spits out one that hasn't.

A guaranteed losing combination. No one wins. The jackpot rolls over. More people play the next time. And then, when they've ripped the arse out of it as much as it can take, they just let it go and the whole cycle starts back up again.

JACKIE. Jesus Mary and Holy Sweet Saint Joseph.

BUSH. So the moral is? Don't do the Lotto unless it's rolled over at least three times. No point.

JACKIE. Bullshit.

FRED. He's convinced me.

JACKIE. That wouldn't be hard.

FRED. I'm never doing it again.

BUSH. Just stick to the rollovers, Freddie.

FRED. No, no, they can piss off now.

BUSH. Wait till it hits a four million minimum.

FRED *snatches the phone. Long pause. Suddenly* FRED *speaks.*

FRED. Sneaky prick.

BUSH (*huge dread*). I can explain.

FRED. Who would have ever thought it?

BUSH. Fred, listen…

FRED. Ronan fucking Collins.

BUSH. Right.

FRED. Of all people.

BUSH. In fairness, I don't think he was ever in on it.

FRED. He wasn't?

BUSH. I don't think so.

FRED. You can't be sure, though.

BUSH. I'm pretty sure.

FRED. Yeah?

BUSH. He was just the front man.

FRED. I suppose.

BUSH. That's all he was.

Pause.

Just a fucking patsy.

JACKIE. Unbelievable.

The doorbell rings. JACKIE *goes to answer it.* CARL *and* GEORGE *enter.*

I have to admit, lads, I was starting to worry.

CARL. No need.

JACKIE. What kept yis?

GEORGE. We went as fast as we could.

CARL. Bit of a hard time finding it.

JACKIE. But find it you did.

GEORGE. Yeah.

JACKIE. Good work, Georgie. I could always rely on you.

JACKIE takes the bag and opens it on the table.

It's empty.

GEORGE. It felt very light alright.

Pause.

JACKIE *(quietly)*. So, where is it?

GEORGE. What?

Pause.

JACKIE. Where is it, Carl?

CARL. Where's what?

Pause.

BUSH. Did you check the side pocket?

JACKIE. I'm looking for Jeremy Beadle again.

GEORGE. That's the way we found it, Jack.

JACKIE. Georgie.

CARL. Only it wasn't where you said it would be, you see. That's what delayed us. It was in the middle of the field behind the hedge. Just sitting there.

JACKIE. Just sitting there?

CARL. In the middle of the field.

JACKIE. All zipped up and empty.

GEORGE. We wouldn't know – we didn't open it.

JACKIE. You didn't open it. That's very good. That's brilliant. Well done.

CARL. Just like you said.

JACKIE. Well, I have to say, lads – you are impressing me now. I mean – hats off – I really thought I had you two down to rights. It just goes to show you. Never in my wildest dreams did I ever think either of you were capable of even conceiving something like this.

CARL. Like what, Jackie?

BUSH. What's going on, George?

GEORGE. Fucked if I know.

JACKIE. Alright now. Fun's over. I'm all out of time and I'm all out of patience. I am genuinely about to stick a broom handle up both your holes and wipe this fucking floor with you, so...

CARL. Jackie, listen...

JACKIE (*screams*). Where's the fucking money?

CARL. Money?

GEORGE. Money?

BUSH. What fucking money?

JACKIE. The money that was in this bag. The money that Fred's fuckwits took from the Securicor van today. The money they hid in the hedge because the little cowardly pricks panicked and thought they wouldn't get back without getting caught.

FRED. They'd good reason, Dad.

JACKIE. My arse. They were kids sent by you to do men's work without any clear instructions how they were to actually do it. I gave you a foolproof little caper to organise and look where we are?

FRED. The law was all over the shop in five minutes flat. They had the scanners. They knew the score. They made a decision based on the facts they had and I really...

JACKIE. What's the difference now anyway? It's a moot point at this stage because the bag is here. The money's not. So I'll ask one last time and I promise I'll see the funny side of this when you bring it in to me – where is it?

CARL. We don't have it, Jackie.

JACKIE (*starting to go for* CARL). Come here, you fat cunt.

BUSH. Jesus Christ.

GEORGE (*very strong*). Don't you lay a fucking finger on him.

JACKIE (*stunned*). Excuse me?

GEORGE. We know our rights and I know how this works, Jack. You're paid. We owe you fuck-all. Not any more. We did what you asked. Got the bag, brought it back, didn't open it and didn't ask questions. Whatever problems you have after that are yours and yours alone. You're not dragging us into it when it's got nothing to do with us. We're out now. So back yourself off.

JACKIE. Do you see this, Freddie?

FRED. I see it.

JACKIE. Take a real close look because this is famous.

FRED. What is?

JACKIE. You are now witnessing the legendary cool of the shark himself. We are staring down the barrel at the poker face of George Bridget Kelly.

BUSH. Bridget?

CARL. Shut the fuck up, Bush.

JACKIE. I'm right, amn't I? My little pudding and pie. You've fallen off the wagon tonight.

GEORGE. I don't know what you're talking about.

JACKIE. You're gambling with me now. You and the Counter here.

GEORGE. I'm finished gambling.

CARL. We both are.

GEORGE. You finished us.

JACKIE. Well, you're back with a bang tonight, boys.

GEORGE. Jack.

FRED. I'll search the car.

JACKIE. Don't bother your hole.

FRED. Give me the keys, Carl.

FRED *takes the keys from* CARL *and leaves.*

JACKIE. High stakes now, my old friend – the very highest, you need to know that. Quarter of a mill – sure – but I'm telling you, I'm warning you now – your very life is on this fucking table. Nothing short of, I promise you that.

GEORGE. We don't have it, Jackie. What more can I say to you?

JACKIE. It's worth it to you, though, isn't it? Isn't it? This particular pot. (*To* CARL.) Sort this shithead out proper. Teach me a thing or two in the long run. You out on top in the end. A real nice prize when you think it through.

GEORGE. Means nothing to me.

JACKIE. You're about to lose here, George. Addict always does. Addict plays to lose. Never leaves the table until it's all gone. No matter how high he goes. Always crashes down. Just becomes a matter of how long he can string his fix out for. A matter of time – that's all. Easiest thing in the world is to beat an addict… Candy from a fucking baby.

GEORGE. You have me in a nutshell, Jack.

JACKIE. I am going to raze you on this, Georgie-Boy.

GEORGE. You do what you have to do. But I won't take it lying down. You hear that. Make sure it's going in your good ear.

JACKIE. Fuck-all wrong with my hearing.

GEORGE. Good – This here is your game we've been playing all night. Not mine. The deck is loaded and I won't stand for it.

FRED (*entering*). No, the car is clean.

JACKIE. Of course the car is clean, Fred. They might be gob-shites but they're not fucking stupid.

A stand-off.

BUSH. For what it's worth, I believe them.

JACKIE. What's that?

BUSH. I believe them, Jackie.

JACKIE. You do, do you?

BUSH. They're telling the truth. Look at them. They have to be.

JACKIE. You're not a gambling man, are you, Bush?

BUSH. Just the Lotto. You know. With the rollovers.

JACKIE. Not a card player, though.

BUSH. No, no interest at all.

JACKIE (*walks behind* BUSH). Just as well.

BUSH. I know.

JACKIE. You haven't the face for it.

BUSH. Don't I?

JACKIE. Too open.

BUSH. Is it?

JACKIE. Too handsome.

BUSH. Really?

JACKIE. And far too fucking friendly.

BUSH. Thanks very much, Jackie.

JACKIE. I'm going to introduce you to a good friend of mine, Bush. I think you two will get on like the proverbial. His name's Stanley.

JACKIE *produces a large Stanley knife.*

GEORGE. Don't you go down this road on me now. This isn't fair.

JACKIE. Little lesson, Freddie, pay attention – The most effective all-round use of the Stanley is the old bash and slash – So first you bash –

He hits BUSH *very hard in the back of the head with the butt of the Stanley knife.*

FRED. Fuck.

BUSH *falls to his knees, jumps right up.*

BUSH. I better be heading off, lads, I'll see yis all tomorrow.

JACKIE grabs him by his hair from behind and places the blade on his cheek just under his eye.

FRED. Game on.

GEORGE. Jackie, Jesus, don't, wait, wait, wait…

JACKIE. Alright, this is it – I'm calling your bluff, lads – You wanted to play – we're playing – Big boys – big pot – big stakes – The rest of the board has checked and I'm all in. I am going to open up his face at the count of three – What's your call, gents? – Look at me, George. Am I bluffing?

BUSH. I don't think he is.

FRED. He's not, George. He's fucking not, so.

JACKIE. Give me a count, Freddie.

FRED. Here we go.

BUSH. No, Fred, Jackie – please – don't.

FRED. One.

JACKIE. Time to fold your hand, lads.

GEORGE. I swear to sweet Jaysus, Jackie.

JACKIE. What's after one, Fred?

FRED. Two.

JACKIE. Now cut your losses, boys – (*Moves the blade to* BUSH*'s throat.*) or I'll cut his fucking throat.

BUSH. Ahh, George.

GEORGE (*picking up the blue bat*). If I see one drop of blood.

JACKIE. Time for the three, son.

FRED. This is going to be terrible messy to clean up.

BUSH. Well, let's just hold on the two for a minute, so.

FRED. Sorry about this, Bush. It's just work, you know. Three.

JACKIE. Say goodnight.

GEORGE. Jackie.

BUSH. Fuck.

CARL. Enough.

GEORGE. Carl – stay out of it.

JACKIE. Come on, Carl – what have you got for me?

CARL. Fuck this, George.

GEORGE. Don't.

CARL. I've done enough. I've caused enough. This has all gone far enough. Forget the field in Tullamore, look where I am now.

JACKIE. Just let it out, Carl.

CARL. I'm sorry, Jackie. I am just about the sorriest prick that ever walked. I am an out-and-out gambling addict and I am officially in the fucking height of it here.

JACKIE. Save it for your meetings. Where's my money?

CARL. I don't have it.

JACKIE (*screams*). Carl.

CARL. I wish I did, Jackie. I really do. But I don't.

BUSH. You better fucking not have, Carl.

CARL. Do you think I'm capable of this, Bush? I could stand here and watch him do this to you? – Do you really think for a minute that I have that in me?

BUSH. I know you don't.

CARL. I'm not made of that, Jackie. I wish to God I fucking was, because if I'd a fraction of it in me I wouldn't be in the state I am today. Look at me. I'm not a player – I'm nothing. I have nothing. I haven't been able to bluff a tenner raise in over a year. I'm a loser now. Bad luck personified and I've brought it down on them. Fucking looks like I've brought it on you too. Well, I'll take responsibility, so whatever you have to do, you do it to me.

JACKIE. Oh – don't worry – I'm going to do all of you – that was the deal. The Three Musketeers – all for you and starting with this prick here.

JACKIE *moves to cut* BUSH. GEORGE *strikes* FRED *hard on the shin with the bat.* FRED *falls to his knees with a scream.* GEORGE *places the bat across* FRED*'s throat from behind and straddles him, holding one end with his hand and the other in the crux of his arm. He is choking* FRED *to death.*

CARL. Jesus Christ, George.

JACKIE. Let him go, George. Let him go to fuck.

GEORGE. He's got less than a minute now, Jackie, and you know it.

JACKIE. I'll kill you for it. Right here in this fucking room.

GEORGE. Maybe, maybe not – I'll take my chances. Your call now.

JACKIE. Stand up, Fred. Get on your feet, son.

GEORGE. He can barely hear you at this stage. Matter of seconds.

JACKIE. You won't go through with it, Georgie – I know you too well.

GEORGE. I'm at your level now, Jackie. You've dragged me down to this tonight.

JACKIE. Bastard.

GEORGE. If we had that money – you'd be fucking welcome to it. You heard Carl – it's that simple. We're not scum,

Jackie – and you'll never turn us into it, no matter how hard you try. Now make your play quickly. The lights are nearly out here.

JACKIE *releases* BUSH *and then* GEORGE *releases* FRED. JACKIE *goes to prepare himself a drink.* FRED *is on the floor on all fours, struggling for breath.* GEORGE *helps him up into a chair.* CARL *goes to help* BUSH.

I'm sorry, Freddie.

FRED. My fucking shin.

GEORGE. I never wanted you to see that from me, son – but I had no choice.

FRED. I'm alright.

JACKIE. We'll be seeing you all very soon, lads.

GEORGE, CARL *and* BUSH *go to leave.*

CARL. Jackie.

JACKIE. What?

CARL. When do I get paid?

JACKIE. Excuse me?

CARL. For the pick-up. Ten grand. We agreed it earlier.

JACKIE. That we did.

CARL. So when, then?

JACKIE. Well, isn't all this absolutely amazing?

CARL. Because the quicker the better with the way things are.

JACKIE. It just goes to show you – doesn't it, Georgie?

GEORGE. What does?

JACKIE. If he had anything to hide from me, anything at all, he would never have had the bollix to stop there and ask me for that money. Right?

CARL. I haven't got anything to hide from you, Jackie.

GEORGE. Neither of us do.

JACKIE. The bag was empty?

GEORGE. That's exactly the way we found it.

JACKIE. You all better fuck off, so.

CARL. But the money, Jackie, because I really could use it.

JACKIE. Take it as credit. In the casino.

CARL. No, no – I'm finished with that now.

JACKIE. Well, go and lose it and you can finish then, okay.

GEORGE. He's not going back near any of it – no matter what.

JACKIE. Please don't push your luck any further, lads. It hasn't been a good day. I'm kind of in the middle of a bit of a situation in case you hadn't fucking noticed.

GEORGE. He's only asking for what is due here.

JACKIE (*loud*). Jesus Christ.

CARL. We'll sort it out some other time, ẙeah.

GEORGE. Hang on a second.

CARL. Let's go, George.

They go to leave again.

JACKIE (*calls*). Carl.

CARL. Yeah.

JACKIE. Come here to me.

CARL *goes to* JACKIE. JACKIE *moves close in, threatening.*

Look me in the eye.

CARL. Okay.

JACKIE. Straight in the eye, Carl, because this is life-or-death time. Nothing short of…

GEORGE. Jackie.

JACKIE. Stay out of this now.

Pause. JACKIE *and* CARL *are nose to nose.*

Lay off the cream cakes.

CARL. I promise.

JACKIE. And start using margarine.

CARL. I will then.

JACKIE. Hate to see you unwell.

CARL. You needn't worry, Jackie. That's my number-one priority.

They leave. FRED *starts to put on his coat and retrieves a weapon.*

JACKIE. Where are you going?

FRED. This is all my mess.

JACKIE. It certainly is.

FRED. So I'm going to go fix it.

JACKIE. And how are you planning to manage that, son?

FRED. It's obvious now, isn't it?

JACKIE. Is it?

FRED. Our little hijack crew of shitheads think they can pull the wool down because I've a reputation –

FRED *picks up the bat.*

JACKIE. What did I ever do to deserve this?

FRED. Well, we'll see how far they last. I'm going over to Kimmage. Back in an hour.

JACKIE. They don't have it.

FRED. Of course they fucking have it.

JACKIE. They couldn't make up a story like that if they tried.

FRED. You think it's still in Tullamore?

JACKIE. Christ Almighty.

FRED. Because I'll go down there now myself.

JACKIE. And what, son? Knock on every house in the town?

FRED. I'll do whatever it takes, Dad.

JACKIE. It just walked out the front door.

Pause.

FRED. No.

JACKIE. And I don't know whether to laugh or cry. Really I
don't, because I have spent my life trying to get that man on
side and he's done nothing but look down his nose at me.
Well, tonight he's lying on a mattress stuffed full of the
hottest money in the country. And he won't sleep a wink. It's
almost too good to be true, if you look at it in a certain light.

FRED. It's not him, Dad.

JACKIE. It's him alright. It's him. It fucking has to be. You
understand me? It has to be. Because I know people. I know
him. Better than any man I've ever known. And I could see
right through him and that fat fuck of his standing there in
front of me.

FRED. But think about it, will you.

JACKIE. Don't talk to me about thinking now, son. Stick to
your strengths and do as I tell you. I want you to stay close
to them. Like superglue. Every move they make. They'll slip
up. And sooner rather than later. Pair of fucking addicts like
them.

FRED. Ahhh, don't go asking me to do that, Dad.

JACKIE. Do what?

FRED. Start hunting down my Uncle George, for fuck's sake.

JACKIE. Your 'Uncle' George, is it?

FRED. It would be a complete waste of time that we just don't
have when we should be focusing on finding who really
robbed us in the first place.

JACKIE. Go over to our friends in Kimmage now. Bring a few lads with you. They deserve what's coming for their incompetence anyway. But you'll see for yourself that they're telling the truth. And you know it's not in fucking Tullamore either. You're not that stupid, are you? Are you, son?

FRED. No.

JACKIE. Good. So then you go and do exactly what I'm telling you with the trio of tossers that just waltzed out of here.

FRED. Jesus.

JACKIE. Because this is all your fault in the first fucking place, Freddie, isn't it?

FRED. Dad.

JACKIE. Isn't it?

FRED. It is, yeah.

JACKIE. And, trust me – you do not need me holding you liable if my money fails to ever show up.

FRED. He would never have done that to me if he had it, though. That much I know for sure. He would have given it up before that.

JACKIE. Well, please don't bet your life on it, son. Let's not let it get that far. You understand?

FRED. I do.

JACKIE. Good.

FRED *makes to leave.*

FRED. I'm sorry about all this messing.

JACKIE. Check in on your mother before you go. See if she wants a cup of tea.

Blackout.

Scene Three

The taxi rank at Dublin Airport. BUSH *is on his phone.*

BUSH. So what's your name? That's quite a stutter you have there, Britney. Oh, it's a stammer, is it? I didn't know there was a difference. Oh no, I like it. It's fucking gorgeous. So tell me – what are you wearing right now?

CARL *enters.*

That's great, Mam. I'll be over to see you soon. Take care. (*Hangs up.*)

CARL. That your mam?

BUSH. Yeah, God bless her.

CARL. She's in Portugal, isn't she?

BUSH. Is she?

CARL. With my ma and Rita. They went out last week.

BUSH. Of course they did. I told her she shouldn't be ringing me. Cost her a fortune.

CARL. How's your head now?

BUSH. Killing me. Fucking lump like a golf ball.

CARL. I feel terrible.

BUSH. Listen – we got off lightly from what I hear. The lads from Kimmage that did the job – he took them within an inch. And it looks like they don't have it either – dead man walking whoever has that money.

CARL. Who was telling you all this?

BUSH. Jasmine. Last night.

CARL. I'm beginning to get worried about you.

BUSH. I'm beginning to worry about myself.

CARL. That type of behaviour. That's compulsive. Obsessive. I know what I'm talking about.

BUSH. I know you do, Carl. I've had to learn that the hard way.

CARL. I'm so sorry, Bush – I went to another GA meeting with George last night.

BUSH. Did you?

CARL. I'm determined now. Get myself right again.

BUSH. Good for you, Carl.

CARL. I had a bowl of Bran Flakes for my breakfast this morning.

BUSH. Seriously?

CARL. I'm starting to feel a bit better about myself. Really I am.

BUSH. You actually look like you've lost some weight.

CARL. Since Wednesday.

BUSH. Yeah.

CARL. Cheers.

BUSH. It might just be that shirt you're wearing.

CARL. Might be just that alright…

BUSH. But you look like you have. In that shirt.

CARL. I didn't weigh myself now, so…

BUSH. Turn around there.

> CARL *proceeds to turn right around.*

> You can definitely see a difference.

CARL. Can you?

BUSH. Definitely.

CARL. That's great, isn't it?

BUSH. You should wear that shirt more often.

CARL. I will, so.

BUSH. Buy yourself a few more of the same.

CARL. Good idea.

BUSH. Oh absolutely.

CARL. See, that's the start. Today's the first day, Bush.

GEORGE *enters*.

BUSH. What happened? – You're only gone.

GEORGE *is silent*.

Was it Swords? Bet you it was Swords.

CARL. Are you okay there, George?

BUSH. You just fuck them straight out the car like I told you.

GEORGE. It wasn't Swords.

BUSH. Malahide? That's worse, nearly, because you've no choice but to take them.

GEORGE. It was Freddie Farrell.

BUSH. What?

CARL. Where?

GEORGE. Waiting for me up on the rank.

CARL. You are joking me?

GEORGE. I'm not, no.

BUSH. What did he want?

GEORGE. He wants his money.

CARL. Oh fuck, George.

BUSH. What does he think you can do about it?

GEORGE. He thinks I can bring it round to his house. Before the day is out.

CARL. I don't believe this.

GEORGE. Or he thinks he is going to have to fucking kill me. So…

CARL. Oh no.

BUSH. Did he actually say that?

GEORGE. Well, from the little I could make out through all of his snot and tears – that's exactly what he said.

CARL. Shit, shit.

BUSH. What did you tell him?

GEORGE. Same as I've told him every other time he's ended up crying on my shoulder. That he's not to worry. It'll all be okay.

CARL. My nerves can't take this.

GEORGE. Well, they're going to have to, Carl. Alright? They can do nothing to each or any of us as long as we don't have that fucking money. And we don't have that fucking money. Look at me. Say it now. Say it.

CARL. We don't have that fucking money.

GEORGE. You too, Bush.

BUSH. Me?

GEORGE. I'm sorry – I wish it wasn't, but it's the three of us in this together, whether you like it or not.

BUSH. I'm cool with it, George – it's a bit of excitement at least.

GEORGE. But you need to know it all, Bush. What we're up against here. We are smack bang in the middle of a face-down now, lads. As soon as they realise we're not blinking because we've got fuck-all to bluff with – it will go away.

CARL. What if it doesn't, George?

GEORGE. It will go away, Carl.

BUSH. Of course it will.

GEORGE. It has to. It has to.

CARL. I'm feeling very hungry all of a sudden.

Pause.

BUSH. They'll find the muppet who has it, Carl, don't worry.

GEORGE. No they won't.

CARL. They're not going to find anything, Bush.

BUSH. Some dozy shithead from Tullamore town will start appearing in snakeskin boots and they'll go through him like a dose of salts.

CARL. That's not going to happen.

GEORGE. Do you understand?

BUSH. Trust me. A fucking biffo with a quarter of a million is going to stick out like a sore thumb.

CARL. It wasn't quarter of a million.

BUSH. Oh, I know what you're saying. It's those fucking banks trying to scam the insurance, isn't it? Inflate the amount taken so the claim back is higher. You know that bank will probably actually make money on this. The insurance company loses out, but what do they do then? – They put up my fucking premium to cover it. Who ends up losing out in the end as always and per bleedin' usual? Me.

Quarter of a million, my arse. Probably around two hundred grand tops.

GEORGE. Two hundred and twenty-four.

BUSH. Sorry?

CARL. And some loose change.

Pause.

BUSH. And how the fuck would youse know that?

GEORGE. We counted it.

Blackout.

The End.

A Nick Hern Book

Rank first published in Great Britain as a paperback original in 2008 by Nick Hern Books Limited, 14 Larden Road, London W3 7ST, in association with Fishamble: The New Play Company, Dublin

Rank copyright © 2008 Robert Massey

Robert Massey has asserted his right to be identified as the author of this work

Cover image by Patrick Redmond; designed by Gareth Jones
Cover designed by Ned Hoste, 2H

Typeset by Nick Hern Books, London
Printed and bound in Great Britain by CPI Antony Rowe, Chippenham, Wiltshire

A CIP catalogue record for this book is available from the British Library

ISBN 978 1 85459 525 6

FSC
Mixed Sources
Product group from well-managed
forests and other controlled sources
Cert no. SGS-COC-2953
www.fsc.org
© 1996 Forest Stewardship Council